CW00553237

Sunderland
Public Houses

by Alan Brett

Two pubs that went to make way for the building of Crowtree Leisure Centre – The George and Dragon (*left*) and the Crow Tree Inn.

Previous page: The Alexandra at Grangetown which dates from before the Second World War. Adrian and Dee Marshall run the pub today as well as the Phoenix Inn at Seaham.

Acknowledgements

I would like to thank the following individuals and organizations for their help with this publication: George Alder, Billy Bell, Tommy Conroy, Bobby Duckworth, John Gettings, Albert Gibbons, Peter Gibson, Dave Gracey, Phil Hall, Billy Hardy, George Hoare, Brian Holden, Bobby Knoxall, Gordon & Beryl Lacy, John Lavelle, Patrick Lavelle, Jack Laydon, John McIvor, Stu McSween, George Nairn, Pat O'Brien, Ken Price, Mary Robinson, Stan Rock, Martin Routledge, John Royal, Jimmy Smith, Tony Smith, Ashley Sutherland, Alan Tedder, Massie Wakinshaw, Trevor Williamson and Ian Wright.

Beamish Museum
Michael Bute
Ian S. Carr
Phil Curtis
Ron Lawson
Matty Morrison
David Moss and daughters Claire, Nicola and Lesley
Sunderland Echo
Sunderland City Library & Arts Centre
Tyne & Wear Museums
Sunderland Museum & Winter Gardens
Newcastle Central Library
Tyne and Wear Archives Service
Vaux Breweries
Ward Philipson

Bibliography

Raich Carter *Footballer's Progress* Sporting Handbooks 1950
Bobby Knoxall *Stand Up!* Ghostwriters UK Ltd 2003
Patrick McLoughlin *The Johnson Street Bullies* New Horizon 1980

Copyright © Alan Brett 2003

First published in 2003 by

Black Cat Publications
163 Brandling Street, Roker, Sunderland
SR6 0LN

ISBN 1 899560 46 7

No part of this publication may be reproduced, stored in a mechanical retrieval system, or transmitted, in any form or by any means, electronic, mechanical, photocopying, recording or otherwise, without prior permission of the author.

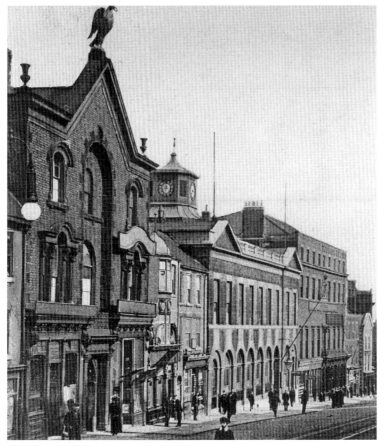

The Eagle, High Street East

From the 1820s this old inn was known as the Exchange Tavern. After undergoing rebuilding work in the 1860s part opened as the Eagle Tavern and the rest as the Eagle Tobacco Factory. The large eagle on the top of the building was a familiar sight to Eastenders (*above*). Edward Newbegin was owner and William Davison the licensee of the Eagle when it was reported to the Compensation Authority (a body that paid for pubs to close) in 1919. In recent years the building has been renovated and a new eagle erected on top.

Half Moon Inn, High Street East

The landlord of the Half Moon, John Snowball, appeared in court in 1854 charged with 'selling liquor in his house on the morning of the General Fast.' Britain had declared war on Russia on 28th March 1854 and a month later a National Fast was held with a day of prayer. The day was almost completely observed in Sunderland with public houses included in those

establishments not opening for trade. Snowball was deemed to have offended unwittingly and was fined 5 shillings and costs. The original inn was converted from a private residence but in 1903 plans were drawn up to rebuild it with an ornate frontage. It closed in 1937 but when it was demolished the Edwardian facade was shipped off to America.

British Empire, High Street East

The Alderman Thompson Arms and Horner's Commercial Hotel were built in 1840 next to the Exchange Building. The hotel was not a success and soon closed but the public house continued with rest of the building being let as offices and shops. The pub changed its name to the British Empire and its doors remained open until 1969. After standing derelict for a number of years (*above*) the building was demolished in 1973.

Quayside Exchange, High Street East

Since its renovation the Exchange Building has opened as licensed premises under the name the Quayside Exchange (*above*).

Grey Horse, High Street East

Formerly called the Fighting Cock Inn it stood a couple of doors up from the Eagle Tavern. In the early 1900s B.F. Simpson, the architect responsible for the design of the neighbouring Half Moon, also drew up plans for the Grey Horse for owners Fenwicks. In 1934 the Grey Horse was deemed by police to be unnecessary and structurally deficient and it was referred for compensation.

Duke of Wellington, Low Street
This eighteenth century tavern in Blue Anchor Yard closed in 1857 – the year from when the OS map (*below*) dates.

Some of the East End riverside pubs shown on the map had gone by the end of the 1850s – The Earl of Durham, Whitwell Inn and Custom House Hotel had all closed by then. All the rest except the Boar's Head and White Swan (the tall building on the skyline) had closed by the 1920s.

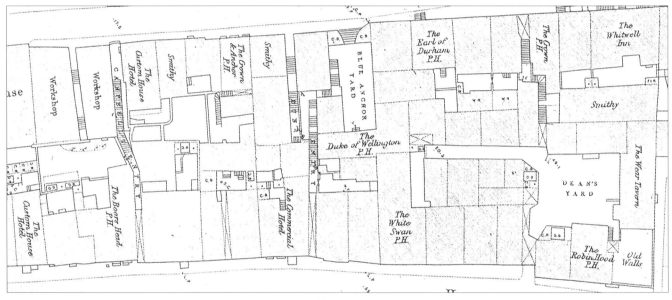

Boar's Head, High Street East
The Boar's Head with dock cranes towering in the background is the only pub on the map that has survived to the present day. In 1792 it had been converted to an inn and was called the Masons Arms. By the 1830s it was known as the Boar's Head.

White Swan, High Street East
On the night of 6th August 1889 German sailors from the barques *Entr'act* and *Johannas* were enjoying their last night on shore at the White Swan before sailing the next day. When the pub closed at 11 o'clock the sailors left but later tried to get back in for more beer. A confrontation with locals left four Englishmen stabbed and three German seamen charged with cutting and wounding. The White Swan closed in 1977 after over two hundred years in business.

Bridge Hotel, Sunderland Street

In the 1790s this was the Sunderland residence of the famous Lambton family. Shortly after the bridge across the river was built in 1796 the building was converted into a coaching inn and named in honour of the new structure. Charles Dickens stayed at the hotel when he appeared at the nearby Lyceum Theatre in 1852. In 1998 landlord Jimmy Byrne was murdered in his own pub and it never reopened. The Bridge Hotel has now been turned into offices and renamed Lambton House after the family who original owned the building.

Richard Stanley Smithson, landlord of the Bridge Hotel in the early 1950s.

Bonded Warehouse, Low Street

The old bonded warehouse at Wylam Wharf was converted into a pub in 2000. Ian Clarke is the current licensee at the Bonded Warehouse.

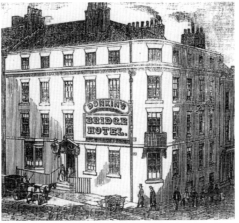

Donkin's Bridge Hotel in the nineteenth century.

The Bridge at the end of the twentieth century.

Lambton House in 2003.

The glazed tiling of the old pub have been retained in the new building.

Royal Standard, High Street East

In 1857 Henry Ray was landlord at the Royal Standard. The 1901 Census records Thomas Swan (34) as a wine merchant manager at the pub. It was one of the last pubs to have spittoons and sawdust on the floor. The Royal Standard is still going strong when many of the neighbouring pubs have closed.

White Lion, High Street East

This pub is recorded as trading in the 1760s. It closed before the Second World War and was being used as a warehouse to store fruit and veg when Hughie Quinn bought it in the early 1980s. He renovated the building and was granted a new licence to reopen the pub. Today the White Lion is again closed and is being converted into flats.

Globe Hotel, High Street East

This eighteenth century hostelry was originally called the Fountain. By the 1820s it was known as the Gardener's Tavern and by 1858 John Chapman was running it. The following year it became the Globe Hotel under Thomas McKenzie. Darlington-born John Ormston (55) was publican at the Globe Hotel in 1901. It closed in 1966 after almost two centuries in business.

Oxford Hotel, High Street East

The Oxford on the corner of High Street East and looking up Church Street (*above*). The Oxford opened its doors for the first time on 1st March 1873 under Helena Rutherford. It had formerly been called the Highlander but was rebuilt in the early 1870s and enlarged by taking over the premises of Olivers the butchers next door. The pub, which originally dated from the eighteenth century, finally closed in 1937.

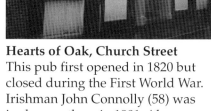

Hearts of Oak, Church Street

This pub first opened in 1820 but closed during the First World War. Irishman John Connolly (58) was innkeeper there in 1901. Almost eighty years after its closure the pub was reopened by Kevin Dobson.

Saddle Inn, High Street East

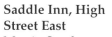

Martin Stephenson, a saddler by trade, bought this tavern in the 1770s. On 3rd May 1853 the old Sunderland custom of perambulating the parish boundaries ended at the Saddle Inn which then hosted a dinner for the dignitaries. At the end of the First World War the old inn closed for the last time.

Ship Inn, High Street East (No. 1)

From the early nineteenth century the pub was known as the Ship Inn. It was popular with ship captains and there was always a room reserved for them there. In recent years this pub has been known as the Corner House and is now the Cavern Bar in honour of the old haunt of the Beatles.

Black Cat, High Street East

Built in the 1960s this pub stands on the site of the Jamaica Vaults. John Churchill was a popular landlord at the Jamaica in the nineteenth century. Every Christmas he gave large quantities of boiled beef, vegetables and bread to needy Eastenders. The Jamaica was demolished when the high rise flats went up and was rebuilt and opened as the Black Cat. *Above:* Licensee of the Black Cat, Michael Bute (with pint), ready to give a rendition of the *Lambton Worm* at the pub in 1981 with George Shovelin (guitar) and Bruce Storey (banjo). A few years later the pub reopened as the East Ender.

Station Hotel, Moorgate Street

The Station Hotel in 1965 (*left*) shortly before its closure. Also in picture are St John's Church and School with the Welcome Tavern in the distance. This pub was named after the terminus of an early railway line that ran nearby. The pub was known as 'Hutchies' after the Hutchinson family who ran the pub for many years. When the Station closed the oldest regular was 83-year-old Mary Blalock of Trafalgar Square. Mary was there the night in 1937 when Sunderland players and officials took the F.A. Cup to the Station. She recalled 'the Cup was filled to the brim with champagne and all the regulars had a drink from it. Then when it was empty, the Cup was filled with beer and we drank that too.'

Left: The F.A. Cup on display outside the Station Hotel in 1937. Licensee Jack Hutchinson (sitting left of the trophy), Dickie Wilkinson the undertaker and Giles Willmott the ratcatcher and father of Shirley (Atta Matta) are just a few of many East End characters in this photograph.

Royal Hotel, Prospect Row

One of the busiest times of the year for this pub was East End Carnival time. A man had to be employed to remain in the cellar all day to change over the beer barrels. When the Royal Hotel's licence was not renewed and referred for compensation in the 1930s the redundant building was bought to replace the old mission of St John's Settlement.

Welcome Tavern, Prospect Row

This pub originally dates from the 1830s but the present building (*above*) dates from 1915. It has survived into the twenty-first century when many around it have not. Since 1991 Geoff and Julie Moon have run the pub.

Butchers Arms, Coronation Street
This pub took the name from the old butchers' market and slaughterhouses in the area. Both the Butchers Arms and its neighbour the Market Hotel first opened in 1834. This was the final pub in Coronation Street to close when last orders were called in 1975.

Market Hotel, Coronation Street
This also took its name from the numerous markets nearby which sold fish, meat, fruit and vegetables, clothes and household items. At one time the Market Hotel was the residence of wealthy businessman John Thornhill. The Market Hotel finally closed in 1971.

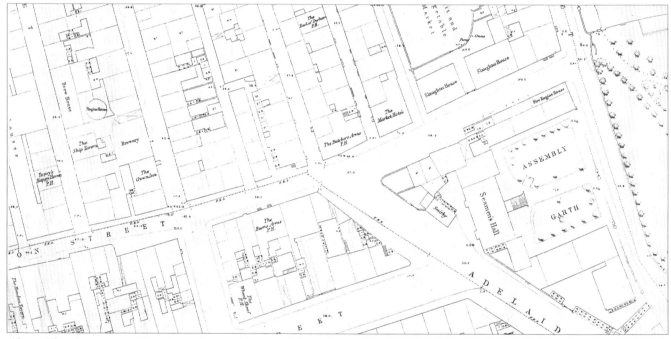

Above: The Coronation Street area in 1857. The Butchers Arms, Market Hotel, Burns Arms (Robert Burns Arms) and Wheat Sheaf are all shown. Topsy's Happy Home in Lombard Street has a claim to the most unusual pub name in Sunderland. Before its closure in 1962 it also had more than its fair share of name changes. In just over a century as licensed premises it was known as: Sloop, William IV, Alnwick Castle, Ship Provident, New Bridge and finally Sunderland Bridge.

Wheat Sheaf, Moor Street
The Wheat Sheaf standing derelict in 2003 with Holy Trinity on the right of picture. The pub dated from 1820 but the old church opened more than a century earlier and has survived when the countless pubs which surrounded it have come and gone.

In 1914 there were a dozen pubs in Coronation Street – *North side*: Engineers Arms (No 6), Dog and Pheasant (13), Grace Darling (17), Holy Island Castle (20), Globe Tavern (34 & 35*), Butchers Arms (54), Market Hotel (55). *South side*: Robert Burns Arms (70), Coronation Bar (83), Temple Bar (90), Meux Arms (92) and Nutwith Hotel (133). Within a decade only half of these pubs remained open.

* The Globe Tavern stood on the corner of Coronation Street and its official address was 20 New Grey Street.

Holy Island Castle, Coronation Street
In the nineteenth century this pub was just one of a number of bars named after castles in the area. There was also the Alnwick Castle and Bamborough Castle in Lombard Street and Tynemouth Castle in Moorgate Street. The Holy Island Castle closed shortly before the Second World War.

Nutwith Hotel, Coronation Street
In the 1840s when this pub was known as the Borough Tavern it was taken over by Robert Ord, a veterinary surgeon and practical horse shoer, whose premises was next door to the pub. The change of ownership was accompanied by a new name – Nutwith was the horse that won the 1843 St Leger at Doncaster. The Nutwith was a casualty of the redevelopment of the Coronation Street area in the early 1960s. A Compulsory Purchase Order in March 1962 was placed on the pub and its price was set at £2,900.

Robert Burns Arms, Coronation Street
Carnival time at the Robert Burns Arms (*left*). John Edward Archibald Pearson was manager of the pub during the First World War and he was there when the photograph was taken. At this time the licensee was John Heaton who had a number of pubs in town including the Welcome Tavern and White Lion. 'Archie' Pearson had been manager of the Alma Hotel in Clark Terrace before taking over the Robert Burns. This was one of four pubs in Coronation Street to close in the early 1920s.

Grace Darling, Coronation Street
On 10th September 1897 a group of men were drinking in the Grace Darling when the question arose of how much a man could drink. Robert Archibold (30) declared that while serving in the Army in India he 'drank many a pint of whisky'. One of the men ridiculed this claim and a shilling wager was suggested. Despite the fact the men had been drinking for four hours a half pint of Irish whisky was ordered and Archibold drank it straight off. He was then taken semi-conscious to his aunt's house where he died. At the inquest the doctor reported the cause of death as 'an overdraught of neat whisky, which caused paralysis of the nerve centres of the brain'. One of the jurymen observed 'Irish whisky is evidently stronger than that supplied to the soldiers in India'. Two weeks after Archibold's death, Rebecca Potts, landlady of the Grace Darling, was fined £5 and costs for selling liquor to a drunken person. At the Licensing Sessions the following August the renewal of the pub's licence was opposed. After the owners reported how the previous tenant had been removed the licence was eventually renewed. However, a decade later the Grace Darling closed its doors for the last time.

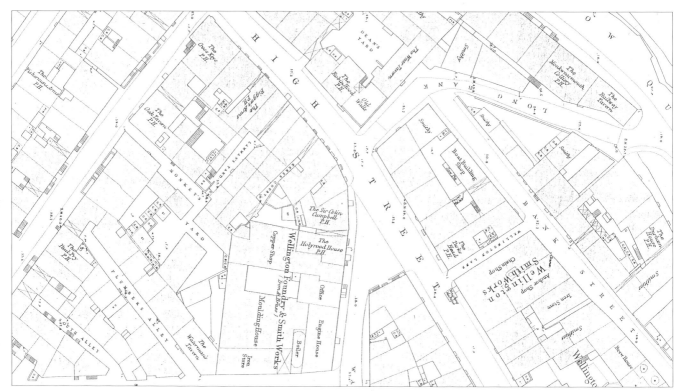

Above: A total of 14 pubs can be seen in this small area of the East End on the 1857 map. Half these pubs around the bottom of High Street had closed by the 1890s.

Waterman's Tavern, Fitters Row
Waterman's Tavern (*above*) before its closure in 1969, the last pub on the 1857 map to go. The building in the background was the Wellington Foundry later used as a warehouse. The last licensee, Jimmy Purdey, used to breed prize bull dogs.

The Adelaide, Adelaide Place
In 1889 when this pub was known as the Jack Crawford it closed for major renovation work. On the night of 2nd May the shored-up building collapsed into a heap of rubble. After being rebuilt its name was changed to the Adelaide. In 1979 the Adelaide was the first Sunderland pub since the 1940s to be referred to the Compensation Authority with a view to closure. Trade had declined to the extent that at its busiest there were less than a dozen customers in the pub. Since its closure as licensed premises it has been a private residence.

Tynemouth Castle, Moorgate Street
Betty Bute's Shipping and General Dealers in Stafford Street (*left*) was at one time the Tynemouth Castle public house (*right*). It closed as a pub in 1920. Betty has deeds for the original building dating back to 1790. Harrison's Buildings, Sunderland's first council houses, stood behind the old pub.

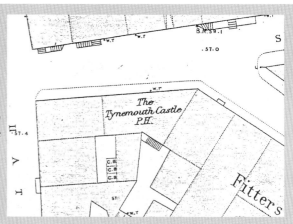

Excelsior Hotel, Lawrence Street

In 1901 Londoner Lydia Brown (57) was hotel keeper at this old beerhouse. In 1988 the pub had a £42,000 refurbishment with licensee Keith Horn and Scottish & Newcastle Breweries each paying half the cost. Despite the makeover Keith was determined to keep going the singalong nights with its resident pianist. The Excelsior is one of the last surviving pubs in this area where the East End sweeps round to meet Hendon.

Dock Hotel, Moor Terrace

Local man Thomas Rendell (28) was publican at the Dock Hotel in 1901. As its name suggests the hotel was near the docks which at one time were one of the busiest in Britain. The Dock Hotel closed in 1959 after more than a century in business.

Swan Hotel, Henry Street

In 1921 the police opposed the renewal of the Swan Hotel's licence because there had been a conviction for permitting gambling on the premises. After the Licensing Magistrates heard it was a very large house doing good trade the Chief Constable withdrew his opposition. It was to remain open for over forty years with last orders finally being called in 1964.

Hendon Station Hotel, East Hendon Road

A view of the Hendon Station Hotel taken on 15th May 1965, only a few years before its closure. This pub stood close to the site of Hendon Railway Station which opened in 1858 and closed in 1879 when Sunderland Central opened. Licensed victualler William Cooper is recorded at the Hendon Station Hotel in the 1901 Census. He was a local man who lived with his North Shields-born wife Sarah and young son at the pub.

Regale Tavern, East Hendon Road

George James took over the Regale in the 1860s and he and his family were still there thirty years later. The Regale Tavern as it looked at the end of the nineteenth century (*above*). Thomas Ratcliffe is the owner of the pub today.

Cottage Tavern, East Hendon Road

This was one of a number of Cottage Taverns which at one time served Sunderland drinkers. After plans were submitted in 1889 the pub was rebuilt. It survived until 1960 when it was demolished in the slum clearance.

Cast Iron & Polly's TO The Mickey Mouse Club

Golden Lion, High Street East
In 1890 the Chief Constable of Sunderland objected to the renewal of the Golden Lion's licence on the grounds that a prize fight had taken place there on 20th May. Police had found a crowd watching two men fighting with gloves on in a ring. The men, from Tyneside, were fighting for a £20 purse. The Licensing Magistrates decided to renew the licence on the understanding that prize fighting did not continue. In the 1930s the pub was used for boxing again, this time legally, when Jack 'Cast Iron' Casey used the premises as his training camp.

The Golden Lion was one of Sunderland's oldest pubs when it closed in 1963. As early as 1755 a group of Freemasons met at the sign of the Golden Lion.

One of Sunderland's greatest fighters of all-time, Jack Casey (light suit), relaxing outside of the ring. When his boxing career was over he tried his hand at pub management at the Theatre Tavern (Polly's) in Lambton Street (*right*).

Theatre Tavern, Lambton Street
This pub was originally going to be demolished in 1954 but had a stay of execution for almost half a century.

Richard Armour (with cat) outside the Hendon Gardens around 1950. His wife, Peggy, was the licensee of the pub at the time.

Hendon Gardens Hotel, Gray Road
For many years this pub had strong connections with the local boxing scene. John 'Pasty' Brown who ran the Hendon Gardens for many years was a great boxing fan. He regularly held social evenings for former boxers. In 2002 the pub was taken over by Anne and Jock Smith and is now called Gray's Inn (*above*).

Ship Inn, High Street East (No. 144)

The 1857 map of High Street East (*below*) shows the old Ship Inn between Bull Lane and Neil's (Neel's) Lane. The pub ceased trading in 1924 and the building now houses Tommy Conroy's newsagency (*right*). The building also houses Sunderland's last surviving professional boxing gym. It underwent a number of name changes in over 150 years as a pub – Hope & Anchor, Royal Oak, Black Lion and finally the Ship Inn. The Mariners Tavern which is also shown on the map did not survive beyond the 1890s.

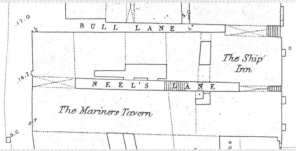

Clarendon, High Street East

This pub stands next door to the former Ship Inn separated by Bull's Lane (*above*). During the Second World War when Matty Robson ran the Clarendon there was an undertaker next door who would sometimes look in and say he needed men to recover bodies from an air raid. Regulars would leave their games of dominoes and pile in the hearse for their grim task.

Left: Tommy Conroy with wife Annette (the first lady boxing promoter in the North East) with some of his early boxers in the gym he built on the back of the former Ship Inn. Sunderland footballers Jeff Clarke and Ally McCoist helped Tommy carry bricks and mix cement for the building that was built overlooking the river in 1984.

Billy Hardy Sports Complex, Baron's Quay Road

Sunderland's greatest fighter of the modern age, Billy Hardy (*left*), has links with pubs. He was for a time manager at the Phoenix at Red House. The boxer also has a licensed premises named after him at Castletown. In 1987 the Billy Hardy Sports Complex opened in the former Hylton Colliery Welfare Ground and the old 'Mickey Mouse Club' became a pub (*above*).

Burlington Inn, Hendon Road

In the winter of 1907, during a time of distress in the town, Tom Innes of the Burlington put on soup and bread for local children. On 5th December he and his wife fed 300 at the Burlington and continued to do so at the same time every week. The Burlington closed in 1957 after serving the local community for ninety years.

Salutation Inn, Hendon Road

The origin of this pub's name could be a shortening of 'The Salutation of the Angel and Our Lady of Grey Friars'. At one time Hendon Road was one of the busiest thoroughfares in Sunderland and the Salutation was one of many pubs which benefitted. In the late 1950s and early '60s the area was radically changed and the Salutation was one of the pubs to close. In 1957 its licence was transferred to the Royal Marine to be built in Sea Road.

The Divan, Hendon Road

This pub was known as the 'Little House' after landlord Tommy Little. He ran trips all over the country so his regulars could watch Sunderland's away games. This nineteenth century pub closed in 1963.

Queen's Hotel, Hendon Road

The old Queen's Hotel (*above*) was known to locals as Charltons after a one time landlord. In the 1980s then landlord Tommy Cooper changed the pub's name to the Charltons (*below*). Tommy's former job was in demolition and one of the buildings he had knocked down was the original Queen's Hotel. The pub was reopened on 12th October 1981 by the Mayor of Sunderland, Tom Finnegan.

Hendon Hotel, Hendon Road
Local man William Boyes (38) was manager at this pub in 1901. He lived there with his wife Margaret and their four children. The Hendon Hotel served its last orders in 1960.

White House, Hendon Road
In the 1900s W.B. Reid & Co used the cellars of the White House to store wines, sherries, ports, liquors and champagne to stock their other pubs in town. The old White House was demolished in 1967 and the newly built pub opened the following year under Jimmy and Maureen Fitzpatrick. When President Jimmy Carter visited Sunderland in 1977 the pub's then landlord wrote to Prime Minister Jim Callaghan inviting The President to Sunderland's version of the White House. Because of the hectic schedule the offer was graciously declined. When George Fraser became proprietor of the White House he renamed it after his grandfather – Gideon. In the summer of 2003 Dave Heron took over and renamed it the Mackem Bar (*above*).

Smyrna Hotel, Smyrna Place/South Durham Street
The Smyrna Hotel on the corner of South Durham Street and Smyrna Place during the 1930s. The old pub closed in the early years of the Second World War.

New Shades, Hendon Road
In 1916 the New Shades was one of the three pubs that were put up for sale following the death of the owner, Arthur Green. It consisted of ground floor bar, snug, front and back sitting rooms and beer cellars. The New Shades closed its doors for the last time on 31st May 1964.

Edinburgh House, Hendon Road
When this pub on the corner of Hendon Road and Fore Street opened in the 1840s Edinburgh was famous for brewing and exporting its ale south of the border. In 1903 alterations were made to the pub's frontage and it did not change much until its closure in 1964.

The Stork, Smyrna Place/North Durham Street
The opening of The Stork on 3rd May 1965 was unusual because at the time the trend was for pubs in this area to close. The first manager in the newly built Nimmo's house was Alexander Fraser (54), who had previously run a number of pubs in County Durham. Today the pub lies derelict (*above*).

Parade Hotel, Hendon Parade

The manager at the Parade from the 1880s until almost 1900 was Walter Smith. He had worked on farms, railways and ironstone mines in his native Northumberland before coming to Sunderland in the 1870s. His eldest son, Walter Jnr, became a barman at the Parade and later succeeded his father as manager. Walter Jnr lived in Hastings Street as there was no living accommodation at the old pub (*left*). The Parade Hotel was rebuilt in the twentieth century (*right*) but was closed in 1996 and eventually demolished.

Lord Roberts, Winchester Terrace

This pub was formerly called the Station Hotel but when it was rebuilt in 1900 at the height of the Boer War, it was renamed after the British Commander in the campaign, Lord Roberts. 'Bob's' closed in 1965 exactly one hundred years after it opened.

International Hotel, International Road

This pub had formerly been Hendon House the residence of the Bramwell family. It was converted into a hotel in the nineteenth century. It was known to locals as 'the Nash' until its closure just before the Second World War.

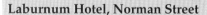

Laburnum Hotel, Norman Street   **Laburnum Cottage, Robinson Terrace**

In 1938 the full licence of the Londonderry Hotel in Surtees Street was transferred to the Villette Club in Robinson Terrace. This club was rebuilt and opened as the Laburnum Cottage. At the same time the licence of the old Laburnum Hotel in Norman Street (*left*) was surrendered. The drinking area of the new pub was larger than that of the two closed pubs combined. The new pub (*right*) is one of the few surviving today in this part of Hendon.

Victoria Hotel, Fore Street

This was another of the many pubs that at one time graced the street corners of Hendon. In 1963 a Compulsory Purchase Order was placed on the pub. Its valuation of £5,566 was one of the highest paid out in Sunderland at that time.

Linden Arms, Linden Street

Alfred Holmes (43) was manager of this beerhouse in 1901. Born in Thornaby, Yorkshire, he was married to a Seaham Harbour girl, Annie. In 1901 they had two sons and two daughters living with them as well as Mrs Holmes' father and another of his daughters, Frances, who worked as a barmaid in the pub. The end for this pub was most unusual as it was knocked down by mistake! During negotiations over the future of the pub between the Council and Whitbread Brewery in March 1971 the contractors, believing (wrongly) the Linden Arms was in the Ward Street Compulsory Purchase Area, went ahead and demolished the building.

The manager of the pub, Roy Morrison, was on holiday at the time and returned to find the pub and the flat above where he lived gone. All that was left for the brewery to do was seek £1,400 compensation for its loss.

Bush Inn, Ward Street

The Bush Inn in the days when it stood on the corner of a terrace street (*left*). In 1901 Sunderland-born James Alexander Alderson (46) was innkeeper at the Bush Inn. He lived at the pub with his wife Elizabeth and son John. They had a domestic servant Emma Cairns from Murton who also stayed at the pub. From the days of the Romans a bush had been a symbol of an inn. Today the pub stands alone and has been renamed the Rovers Return (*right*).

Prince of Wales, Hill Street

This small pub comprised only a bar and room. In 1901 Durham-born Frederic J.B.

Wade was recorded as the beerhouse keeper at the bar. Dating from the 1870s the Prince of Wales closed in 1963.

Oddfellows Arms, Fowler Street

This nineteenth century pub was known by locals as the 'Monkey House' and closed in 1961.

Londonderry Hotel, Surtees Street

Dating from the 1860s the licence of this pub was transferred to the new Laburnum Cottage in 1938. The compensation value was around £1,800.

Three Tuns, Moor Street
In 1901 Bishop Auckland man Joseph Miller (64) ran the Three Tuns with the help of his son, Alfred. The old pub closed in 1959 after almost a century of trading.

Alma Hotel, Clark Terrace/Railway Street
This pub on the corner of Clark Terrace and Railway Street was named after a battle in the Crimean War. After just over a century in business the Alma closed in 1960.

Trimmers Arms, Moor Street/Pemberton Street
On the afternoon of 17th May 1905 police raided the Trimmers for illegal betting. Those in the pub at the time were taken to the police station for questioning. Despite this brush with the law the Trimmers remained open until 1960 – just before off-course betting was legalized with the opening of betting shops.

Maple Bar, Ford Street
Tommy Hazard, who ran the Maple in the late 1950s until its closure in 1963, used the pub's yard as a scrapyard. He had a set of scales set up and would buy scrap from local men. Much of this scrap was brought in on the tide at a groyne near Hendon Docks.

In the early 1930s young Albert Gibbons used to deliver meat for his father by horse and cart. When he was finished he used to go down the docks with his schoolmates and load up with sawdust from the timber yards. They then went round the local pubs and sold the sawdust for bar floors at 6d a bag.

Bath Hotel, Moor Street/Lawrence Street
The landlord of the Bath Hotel was the first in Sunderland to be taken to court under the Intoxicating Liquors (Sales to Children) Act 1901. On 15th January 1902 Thomas Stoker Joyce appeared in court charged with knowingly supplying a girl of under 14 years of age. The girl was stopped by a policeman coming out of the pub and when asked what was in the can she was carrying replied 'A pint of Burton beer for a man working on a truck'. She had told the landlord she was 14. However, it was later found out she was only 11 but as her face was dirty and hair unkempt she looked older. The case against the Bath's landlord was dismissed but the man who had sent her for the beer was fined 5 shillings. The name of this pub recalls the area's former claim to fame as a Spa resort. Between 1820 and 1840 visitors went to Hendon for bathing and many stayed at the Bath Hotel. The pub finally closed in 1957 and was demolished in the slum clearance.

The Alexandra, Queen Alexandra Road
Built just before the Second World War, the pub's large ballroom has hosted dances, presentation functions and even indoor bowls. In 1985 the pub was refurbished with an American theme and renamed Porcupine Park. It has now returned to its former name under Adrian and Dee Marshall.

The Rosedene, Queen Alexandra Road
In February 1961 the Corporation Planning Committee approved an application by Vaux and Associated Breweries for the change of use of the mansion, Rose Dene, to become a public house.

Strawberry Cottage, Tunstall Lane
Darlington-born John Thomas Johnson (59) was innkeeper and market gardener at Strawberry Cottage in 1901. He lived there with his American wife Mary (49) and two Sunderland-born sons. Only a couple of years after the 1901 Census was taken it ceased trading as a pub. *Above*: Seen shortly before its demolition in 1958.

Tunstall Lodge, Burdon Lane
This hotel opened in 1987 in the former residence of Andrew White, Sunderland's first Mayor in 1836. The Grade II listed building, dating from 1760, cost £200,000 to renovate.

The Ashbrooke, Stannington Road
This Scottish & Newcastle Breweries' house opened on 6th September 1967 under the management of Orston Watt who had formerly run the Victoria Gardens.

Hollymere, Leechmere Road
Built in 1991 the Hollymere offers a wide range of entertainment including live music, karaoke and quiz nights.

The Sandcastle, Ryhope Road
This pub has a Wacky Warehouse attached to ensure children have plenty to keep them entertained while their parents are having a drink.

Inn Place, Knollside Close
This Mill Hill pub opened its doors for the first time in 1985 in the premises of a former workingmen's club.

Doxford Lad, Jimmy Carter Centre
This was the first pub built in Sunderland by John Smith's Brewery. It was opened by Mayor Tom Bridges on 8th September 1977 and run by John and Pat Grant.

Blue House, Commercial Road/Corporation Road

In 1898 the original pub was put up for sale with the 'option or privilege of building within 12 months a hotel on a new free site at the corner of Corporation Road and Commercial Road in substitution for the present site of the Blue House Inn'. The nearby Blue House Field was Sunderland AFC's first ground in 1879. The owner of the pub today is Billy Jones.

Victoria Gardens Hotel, China Street

In 1901 Gateshead-born Harry Stephenson (41) was innkeeper at the Victoria Gardens Hotel. The pub is still going strong in 2003 almost a century and a half after it first opened.

Hendon Grange Hotel, Ocean Road

This pub was named after Hendon Grange Farm which occupied the area before housing development in the 19th century. Its address refers to the German Ocean, the former name of the North Sea, which the pub overlooks.

Salem Hotel, Salem Street

In 1938 Cameron & Co, owners of the Salem, received approval for extensive alterations to the pub. Having acquired the premises next door, the pub was almost totally rebuilt. In November 1988, after a £140,000 refurbishment the pub reopened as the Tap and Spile. The Victorian decor was complemented with traditional pub games such as shove ha'penny and bar skittles. The pub is now called the Tap and Barrel.

Rink Hotel, Hudson Road

After opening in 1879 this was a popular bar as it lay just off the town centre between Hendon and the East End. The pub's name was changed to Strokes after a hundred years trading as the Rink. Strokes closed in April 2002 and after a number of fires the old pub was demolished in March 2003.

Tatham Arms, Tatham Street

This pub was called the Crown Stores until undergoing a major revamp in the mid 1930s. Until 1935 the pub could not open on a Sunday as it only had a six day licence. The seven day licence of the Fitzroy Hotel, Wilson Street, Monkwearmouth, was sacrificed and transferred to the Tatham. Despite these improvements the Tatham Arms closed in 1968.

The Bedford Street/Lambton Street Redevelopment Scheme saw the demolition of three pubs at a stroke. The Rose and Crown (Garrick's Head), Cooper's Bar (Theatre Tavern) and Cee Pee's (Caledonia) were all levelled to the ground in the summer of 2003. The Imperial Vaults had gone a few years before. Plans for the area include a cinema complex and ironically some of the pubs that made way for this had strong connections with the theatre district of the nineteenth century. The Theatre Tavern was named after the nearby Lyceum Theatre and the Garrick's Head was named after the famous actor David Garrick. There was also the Cafe De L'Europe adjoining the Theatre Royal in Bedford Street and a Kean's Head down in Spring Garden Lane named after another famous thespian, Edmund Kean.

The Caledonia, Lambton Street
Tony and Brenda Thubron outside the pub they ran for 27 years until their retirement in 1978. In the days when most pubs' last orders were 10.30 pm the Caledonia's was 10 pm. It did not sell spirits until 1979 having had until then a licence to sell ales, wine and cider only.

Above: Garrick's Head (although with an unusual spelling), Bedford Street. This pub closed as the Rose and Crown but had previously been known as Pharaoh's, Mr Smith's and the Crown.

Right: Theatre Tavern, Lambton Street. It was also known as Cooper's Bar and Polly's.

Below left: The Caledonia, Lambton Street. Formerly The Cally, Quavers and Cee Pee's.

Below right: Imperial Vaults, Lambton Street. The first of these pubs to be demolished.

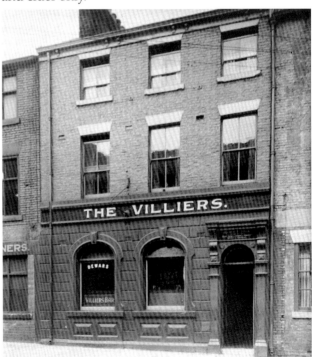

Villiers Hotel, Villiers Street
The Villiers was one of John Vipond's many pubs in Sunderland in the early 1900s. In the 1950s and '60s Norwegian Edwin Torgensen and his wife Frances ran the Villiers with the help of their daughters Agnes, Elizabeth and Farina. Agnes ran the Saltgrass at Deptford in the early 1960s. The Villiers closed in the early 1970s but the building has survived and is now used as business premises.

Johnny & The Turf TO The Carters & Strattons

Johnny Campbell, one of the outstanding players in Sunderland's early history, was later the manager of the Turf Hotel in Bedford Street. After signing from Scottish club Renton in 1889 he went on to become the most feared centre-forward in England. He was a member of 'The Team of All the Talents' and played in Sunderland's first ever League match in 1890. Johnny was a key member of Sunderland's first three League championship sides, finishing top scorer in the 1891-92, 1892-93 and 1894-95 title-winning seasons. After finishing his career at Newcastle he became a licensed victualler and returned to Sunderland to take over the Turf Hotel. It was here he was taken ill and died on 8th June 1906 aged only 36. He had been at the Turf about 3½ years. Large crowds gathered in Bedford Street and West Wear Street to pay their last respects to one of the Sunderland Greats.

Queen's Hotel, Fawcett Street
The Annual Meeting of the Football League was held at the Queen's on 13th May 1892 and it was to prove a memorable occasion. Sunderland were formally presented with the championship trophy they had won in the 1891-92 season (the first of their six titles). Johnny Campbell and his team-mates were presented with specially struck gold medals to mark their achievement. The meeting at the Queen's also saw the formation of a Second Division and an enlarged top flight with the inclusion of Newton Heath (later to become Manchester United). The Queen's closed in 1924 and Woolworths now stands on the site of the old hotel.

James Potts Henderson, Sunderland AFC's first chairman and the driving force in the club's relocation to Roker Park in 1898, was a prominent pub owner. The family's wine and spirit business had been started by his father in the 1860s. After his father's death the company was carried on by James Jnr and James Potts Henderson. The crown jewel of Henderson and Sons was The Bells public house (*above*) on the corner of Bridge Street and West Wear Street.

THE

THE BEST
SPIRITS & WINES

Schweppes
Mineral Waters.

Bass' Ales.

Champagne
on draught.

Selected Cigars.

BOVRIL.

NEXT TO NEW ARCADE,

HIGH STREET, SUNDERLAND

J. W. FLINN, Proprietor.

An advert for the Fountain Hotel from 1902.

Billy Hogg

Fountain Hotel, Frederick Road
Sunderland and England forward of the early 1900s, Billy Hogg, became a licensed victualler on hanging up his boots. After running pubs in Earsdon and West Stanley he moved back to Sunderland in the 1920s to take over the Fountain Hotel in Frederick Road. After a spell as trainer at Roker Park he returned to pub life at the Old Mill Inn at Southwick. One story his regulars would never tire of hearing would be the time Billy scored a hat-trick in Sunderland's 9-1 victory at Newcastle in 1908. The Fountain Head/Hotel, also known as the Frederick Hotel, closed in 1943.

When Raich Carter was invited to pull the first pint at the newly built Colonel Prior on 11th May 1983 it was by no means the first experience the Sunderland legend had with the pub trade. Raich's father, Robert 'Toddler' Carter, ran the Ocean Queen pub in Tower Street in Hendon before the First World War. He too had been a professional

footballer having played for Burslem (later Port Vale), Fulham and Southampton. Raich spent his childhood at the pub and later recalled how Sunderland stars of the day like Charlie Buchan would call in for a chat with his father. Raich's mother's family were also in the pub trade. His grandfather

Colonel Prior, Moorside Road
This Doxford Park pub was named after Colonel Joe Prior (*right*), Sunderland AFC chairman in the 1940s who had lived nearby. In his autobiography *Footballer's Progress* Raich Carter recalled Colonel Prior as a great character. 'One of the old school. He was a typical country squire with stovepipe trousers, a large cravat, and a loud voice. He was a man who could laugh about defeat.'

Horatio Stratton (after whom he was named) was licensee at the Burton House in Hendon for over thirty years. He was also for a time manager at the nearby Waverley Hotel and Blue House Hotel as well as being involved in local football in the early days of Royal Rovers.

Burton House, Fowler Terrace/Norman Street
On the death of his father in 1935 Fred Stratton took over the Burton House maintaining the family tradition in the licensing trade. The pub finally closed its doors for the last time in 1961.

Not far from where Fred Stratton's Burton House once stood is the Bush in Ward Street where former Sunderland winger Tommy Reynolds was manager for a time in the 1960s. Over the years many Sunderland players have gone into the pub trade after retiring from the game. When former Sunderland defender Richard 'Dickie' Ord took over the Royal George in Old Shotton in 2003 he said 'I'm told all ex-professional footballers end up running pubs, so I thought I'd give it try.'

Rising Sun, Trimdon Street
Sunderland full back and team-mate of Raich Carter in the 1937 F.A. Cup-winning side, Jimmy Gorman, ran the Rising Sun in the 1940s. It was one of eight pubs in Sunderland bearing this name over the years. This Rising Sun closed in 1963.

Norfolk House, Norfolk Street

The old Norfolk House building in 2003. The pub dating from the 1870s had a new lease of life after it closed at the end of the 1960s. Sunderland Merchant Navy Association took it over at the end of 1968 and reopened it as a club in July 1969.

Local man William Bell (39) was manager at this pub in 1901. He lived there with his wife Jane Ann and their six children. Also part of the household was William's widowed sister-in-law, Hannah Allan, who worked as a domestic servant. In the 1950s one of the attractions of this pub was comedian Bobby Knoxall. The manager of the Norfolk Hotel (as it was then known) asked Bobby to organize the entertainment on Tuesday and Thursday nights. He would take to the stage himself to sing and went on to form a band called the Rock n' Roll Boys which had Ronnie Sweeney on saxophone. More of his time on stage was spent telling jokes than singing and it was as a comedian that he became famous around the world. In 2003 Bobby Knoxall's autobiography *Stand Up!* was published which tells of his life in show business.

Bobby Knoxall (*centre*), Louis Lebihan (*left*) a local builder and Ronnie Sweeney (*right*) in the Norfolk in the 1950s.

Burton House, Borough Road

In March 1983 the Burton's landlord, Sammy Doran, offered a new drink behind the bar – milk! Milk is no longer available there but the traditional brews are. In 1998 the pub underwent a £200,000 refurbishment. One new feature being the wood flooring reclaimed from the old Roker Park football ground.

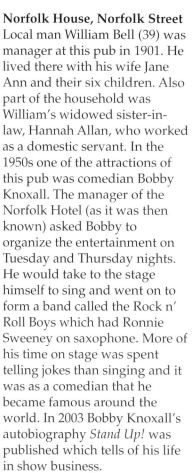

Blondies, West Sunniside

This bar was opened in 1986 by Dave Brogan. The premises is now a restaurant.

Windsor Castle, Nile Street

In the nineteenth century this pub was known as the Criterion. After the General Post Office was built in nearby Sunniside it was renamed the Post Office Restaurant. Despite another name change to the Windsor Castle many people continue to call it the Post Office. Today the licensee is Brian Cooper brother of Tommy who formerly ran Charltons and Cooper's Bar (Theatre Tavern).

At one time, apart from the Windsor Castle, there were three other pubs in Nile Street. At No 20 was the Havelock Hotel. It had started out in the nineteenth century as the General Havelock but had dropped the General well before its closure in 1969. The Lord Nelson Hotel at No 43 was known as the Freemen's Arms in 1834. It closed before the Second World War. In the 1870s the Bodega was at No 65. In the 1890s there was a name change to the Hertford Hotel. It was under this name that it closed in 1967.

The Bells, Bridge Street/West Wear Street
As the nineteenth century drew to a close Henderson and Sons decided the old Bells public house needed a radical modernization. After major reconstruction around 1900 the Bells was soon holding dinners, Masonic banquets, ball suppers and wedding breakfasts. The Bells closed on 26th November 1961 to make way for road improvements and was demolished in the summer of 1962.

The Central, Bridge Street
When this pub was put up for sale on 31st May 1910 it had problems in attracting a new owner. When bidding reached £17,400 it was declared sold. When the purchaser failed to pay the deposit the auctioneer offered the pub to the next highest bidder. When he declined the offer the sale began again. Finally W.B. Reid & Co of Newcastle bought the property for a bargain price of £16,400. In November 1979 an £80,000 renovation converted three downstairs rooms into one with the decor incorporating a railway theme. For years the pub's location near the north end of the old Central Station meant it was popular with rail travellers. The Central survived while many of its neighbours were being demolished and is now known as the City Tavern.

Rowland Burdon Arms, Bridge Crescent
Rowland Burdon was the man who put up most of the money to build the original Wearmouth Bridge in 1796 and gave his name to the pub overlooking it (*seen below on the 1857 map*). When the police objected to licence renewals they normally complained there were too many pubs in the vicinity.

However, in February 1925 Superintendent Ruddick objected to the renewal of the Rowland Burdon Arms in Bridge Crescent as it was 'off the beaten track'. The owners said the pub would have a more important position when the new bridge was completed. Unfortunately the pub did not survive to see the completion of the new bridge in 1929.

Argo Frigate, West Wear Street
This pub dating from the 1820s stood across the road to the Turf Hotel. The pub closed in July 1971 with Betty Heskett being the last licensee.

Turf Hotel, Bedford Street/West Wear Street
The Turf Hotel seen on the 1857 map (*right*). Mark Dixon and daughter Florrie Cairns at the Turf Hotel (*below*). Florrie was the pub's last manageress having taken over from her father who had ran the Turf for 27 years before a fall forced his retirement. The Turf was run as a real family affair with Florrie's mother, Flo Dixon, and Mr Dixon's niece, Bessie Pinkney, helping out. The Turf closed its doors for the last time on 27th March 1960.

Blandford House, Blandford Street

This beerhouse was offered at auction in October 1890 when it consisted of 'capital bar, sitting room and kitchen; sitting room and two bedrooms upstairs; first-class cemented cellar, washhouse, yard and conveniences.' Trade fixtures and fittings were included in the sale and these comprised: counter, beer pumps, Venetian blinds and gas fittings. Today the pub is still going strong in this busy pedestrian precinct in the city centre.

Brougham Arms, Brougham Street

This pub started life in the 1840s. In 1901 Welshman Edward Davies (58) was manager of the pub. Elsie Peterson (*below*) was manageress for the last three years of the Brougham's life. It closed on 27th January 1963 and was demolished shortly afterwards as part of Sunderland's Central Area Redevelopment Scheme. The pub's regulars did enjoy its last night – the beer was free!

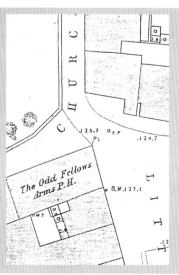

Walworth Castle, Walworth Street

Early in the nineteenth century George Harrison inherited land near Crowtree Road. His son bought Walworth Castle near Darlington and named the pub and street after it. Although the pub closed in 1954 it was to be a number of years before the new town centre redevelopment was complete. Walworth Way is the last link with the name today.

Upper Deck, Walworth Way

The Upper Deck opened on 2nd July 1969 and was named after its location on the first floor of the pedestrian walkway above the town centre shops. Mavis Whitfield was the first manageress of this Scottish & Newcastle Breweries' pub which was decorated with a nautical theme. Although the Upper Deck only existed for twenty years it was one of the most popular town centre bars. An unusual feature of the pub was that it was just as busy during the day as at night. It had to close to enable the roof to be put on The Bridges shopping centre.

Oddfellows Arms, Church Lane

The Oddfellows Arms on the corner of Church Lane and Littlegate near Bishopwearmouth Green seen on the 1857 map. By 1889, when it was put up for sale, it was known as the Cyprus Hotel. It was advertised as having a 'capital cellar underneath' and 'above are two large and lofty rooms, one suitable for a lodge room or billiard room.' In 1935 Frank Lancelot Robson had the licence of the Cyprus Hotel transferred to the new Grange Hotel on Newcastle Road.

Grand Hotel, Bridge Street

An advertisement from 1912 describes the Grand Hotel as 'one of the finest in the North of England, and has a commanding and airy situation in Bridge Street. It was recently redecorated and refurnished and, as it stands, represents the last word in luxury, elegance, convenience and service. It has electric light through-out, perfect sanitation, a comfortable lounge and large and magnificently furnished public rooms. Magnificence has not been paid for by sacrifice of comfort. The ventilation and heating are the acme of studied perfection, and the cuisine and wine list are everything that can be desired by the most fastidious tastes.' The Grand Hotel finally closed in 1969 and was demolished and now Bridge House offices occupy the site.

Empress Hotel, Union Street

This hotel had a prime location beside the railway station until it was badly damaged in an air raid in the Second World War and had to be demolished. In 1901 an Australian lady, Anne Jackson (37), was manageress at the Empress.

Walton Hotel, Fawcett Street

Eleanor Bland (40) from York was manageress at the Walton Hotel in 1901. She ran the hotel with the help of her sister Blanche and ten servants. There were four guests on the night of the 1901 Census, three of whom were commercial travellers. The Walton Hotel's location opposite the Town Hall was a major problem – the clock's chimes kept guests awake at night. It closed as a hotel and opened as Laing & Company's Bar later known as The Vestry. The Laing family owned this bar and the 'Tea Shop' in High Street West from the end of the nineteenth century until 1961 when they were sold to the brewery Hammond Charrington. As a result of this takeover the bar opened on Sundays for the first time in 1963. The manager at the time, Jack Waters, said he and his staff took a while to get used to opening on the Sabbath. It was also one of the last pubs in Sunderland to allow women in. It later underwent a radical make over and changed its name to Christies and Fifth Avenue. After being closed for a number of years this famous Fawcett Street bar is due to reopen on 5th December 2003 as the Old Vestry with an extension to the premises planned at the turn of the year.

Laing & Company's Bar, Fawcett Street, in 1962.

Palatine Hotel, Borough Road

In the 1830s these premises were no more than a thatched cottage known as the Gardener's Tavern. In the next decade, after major rebuilding work, it was renamed the Mowbray Arms. In the 1890s further reconstruction was carried out accompanied by another name change to the Palatine Hotel. Sheffield-born Samuel Fletcher (36) was the Palatine Hotel manager in 1901. He was a widower and lived there with his four children. His housekeeper was Annie Sinclair from Sunderland who the Census described as 'about 40'. The twentieth century saw large amounts of money spent on a number of modernizations and a return to the name Mowbray Park Hotel.

Black Bull, High Street West

This eighteenth century pub dates from a time when Bishopwearmouth was a separate township from

Sunderland. The Black Bull as it looked in the early 1900s (*right*) when it was a Robert Deuchar house. In recent years it has been known as Scott's and the Outpost but has now reverted back to its original name.

George and Dragon, High Street West

The building of the People's Palace Theatre next door in 1891 signalled major refurbishment in the pub itself. After the work was complete it boasted a billiard saloon with five tables. Plans for the building of the Leisure Centre led to the closure of the George and Dragon in 1973.

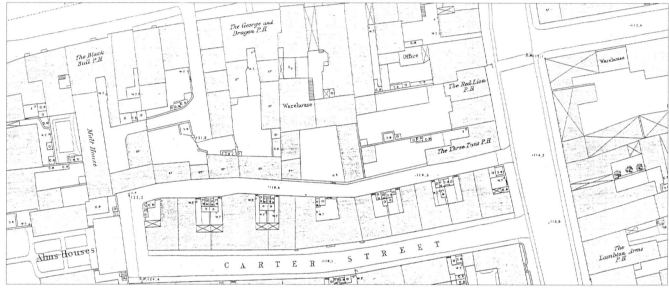

Above: Of the five pubs shown on the 1857 map only the Black Bull survives today. The Crow Tree Inn is not shown because it did not open until the 1870s.

Right: Three pubs in a row in Crowtree Road: Crow Tree Inn, Three Tuns and the Red Lion. On the night of the 1901 Census the Crow Tree Inn was occupied by barman William Forrest (29) and housekeeper Jessie Bedford (36); no one was staying in the Three Tuns; and at the Red Lion lived manager John Dugdale (40) and his family. The building of the Leisure Centre led to the closure and demolition of all three nineteenth century pubs in the early 1970s.

Lambton Arms, Crowtree Road

This pub was fortunate to survive the air raid of 16th May 1943. The King's Theatre which stood next door was destroyed in the raid although the derelict building (*seen left*) remained for another decade before it was demolished. The Lambton Arms closed in 1960 as the area was prepared for the new town centre redevelopment.

Old Twenty Nine, High Street West

Formerly known as the Boilermakers Arms this pub was revamped in the 1970s and renamed the Old Twenty Nine after its number in the street. Its new lease of life was not to last as it closed and was demolished at the end of the 1980s.

In the early 1900s the Corporation had plans to redevelop the area around the top of High Street West. In 1901 both the Londonderry Arms and the Dun Cow were rebuilt. The Corporation sponsored competitions in 1902 for designs for new Law Courts, Police Station and Fire Station. These buildings were completed five years later together with the Empire Theatre.

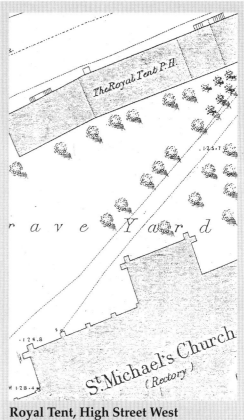

Royal Tent, High Street West

This pub was one of a row of buildings in front of Bishopwearmouth Church (*seen on the 1857 map*). Because of its location the pub was known as the 'Hole-in-the-Wall'. It closed in 1928 and was demolished to allow the top of High Street West to be widened.

Dun Cow, High Street West

This was one of only two Sunderland pubs singled out by the Campaign for Real Ale (CAMRA) in 2003 as being of special historic interest. Its location opposite the Sunderland Empire makes it a natural watering hole for acts appearing there. These have ranged from Hollywood stars such as Howard Keel to pantomime performers. After a period as Rosie's Bar it has now reverted to its traditional name.

Londonderry Hotel, High Street West

Formerly known as the Peacock Inn it was at one time Bishopwearmouth's principal coaching inn. By 1834 it was known as the Londonderry Arms after the local landowner. The pay for a barmaid at the Londonderry in 1909 was 18 shillings a week. We know because it came out in a court case regarding unfair dismissal. The barmaid in question had every third Sunday off but when this fell on Easter Sunday (one of the busiest days in the year in the pub trade) and she did not turn in she was sacked. The first floor of the building now houses a 1970s style bar called Flares.

Bee Hive, Holmeside

The old Bee Hive (*left*) prior to a radical rebuild in the 1960s (*right*). It retained its original name but has since gone through many different names including – The New City, Maggie May's, Huxters and now Savannah.

Park Inn, Olive Street

After going through an Irish theme pub phase as Kitty O'Shae's this old hostelry returned to its traditional name but has recently had another makeover and is now Bar Pure.

Laing's, Olive Street

Opened as Gatsby's on 29th October 1987 after the film and book *The Great Gatsby*. It changed its name to Bunnies in 1990 but is now called Laing's.

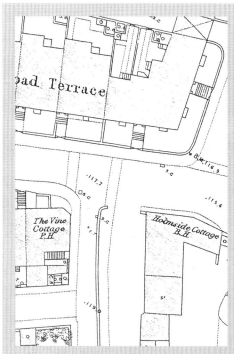

The Borough, Vine Place

When this pub opened in the 1820s it was called the Vine Cottage. It was still known as this in 1857 (*left*). (The Holmeside Cottage on the corner facing closed in 1900.) By 1871 it had changed to the Borough. The pub underwent a large scale refurbishment in 1985 returning to a Victorian theme.

Continental Hotel, St Thomas Street

In the late 1870s Ann Jackson was innkeeper at the Alexandra. The basement bar was later renamed the Baltic Chambers. The pub was one of the casualties of the air raid of 14th March 1943 on the town centre. When the foundations were being dug for the new pub workmen found 90 bottles of red wine and 20 half bottles of white wine which had been buried under rubble on the night of the raid. The new Continental Hotel opened on 1st

August 1958 and consisted of a buffet and snack bar in the basement, lounge and cocktail bar on the ground floor and assembly hall and cocktail bar on the first floor. In 1988 the pub had a radical makeover with shops replacing the ground floor area leaving a first floor bar renamed Gillespies.

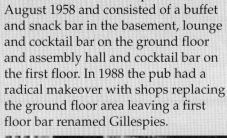

Above: Barmaids at the Continental in the 1960s, with Lily Brett (right).

Top left: Public houses were not a priority in the post-war rebuilding programme and it was not until 1958 before the new Continental Hotel opened.

Left: Gillespies with shops now on the ground floor.

The Refreshment Rooms, Sunderland Railway Station

The Refreshment Rooms was the name by which this bar was known to the Licensing Magistrates although most people knew it as the Bricklayers Arms. It began trading when the Central Station opened on 4th August 1879. Situated at the north end of the station, there was a two-bedroom apartment for the Refreshment Room-keepers.

When the station was given a major facelift in the 1960s the bar was relocated. The new Refreshment Rooms on 2nd September 1966 (*right*). Note the Sunderland football team pictures on the wall. Football special trains taking supporters to away games left from the station. The new version of the Refreshment Rooms closed in the 1980s.

Hat and Feather Vaults, Low Row
In the early 1900s this was one of the pubs owned by Arthur Green. In the 1970s the pub changed its name to 'The Greens' then it was called Ye Olde Transporter and is now back to the Greens.

Queen's Head, Low Row
When this pub was put up for sale in September 1883 it was occupied by John Cowell and was 'most advantageously situated for trade … comprising a convenient and spacious dwelling house, containing 10 good fire-rooms, cellars etc with a spacious yard behind the same.' Having first opened its doors for business in the 1790s the Queen's Head finally closed in 1963.

Plough Inn, Low Row
Right: The Plough Inn (on the left of the white building) around 1875, with Bishopwearmouth Church in the background. The police opposed the renewal of the Plough's licence in 1894 because the licensee had been fined 40 shillings the previous November for selling intoxicating drinks to a drunken person. The Licensing Magistrates renewed the Plough Inn's licence but it was to remain open only another dozen years before closing for good.

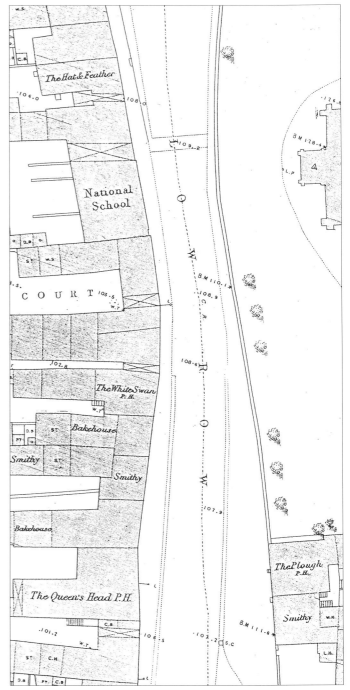

Above: Low Row in 1857, the eighteenth century White Swan public house closed in the decade following the map's publication.

Lambton Worm, Low Row

This J.D. Wetherspoon pub opened in 2003 and was named after the local legend. The first J.D. Wetherspoon pub was opened in 1979 by Tim Martin and by 2003 his company ran 638 pubs in Britain. The pub chain was named after a former schoolteacher of Martin's and the initials came from J.D. Hogg from the *Dukes of Hazard* television series.

Envy, Green Terrace

Envy in Green Terrace was opened by Kevin Dobson in December 2002. Eric Robson is now licensee with Bev Doran as manageress. A name change to Vision is planned for November 2003.

Fitzgeralds, Green Terrace

A view of Fitzgeralds in the summer of 2003. Although this pub only dates from 1981, when it opened as Greensleeves, the building itself dates from the eighteenth century when it was owned by a Quaker family the Richardsons who owned nearby tanyards and flour mill. In October 2003 Fitzgeralds was named North East Pub of the Year by CAMRA.

Baroque, Low Row

This was one of the last bars to open in Sunderland in the twentieth century. It forms a row of four pubs next to each other in Low Row. This is a throwback to the 1850s when a similar number of licensed houses flourished in Low Row. The Hat and Feather (Greens) is the only survivor from that period.

Victoria's, Low Row

It took just 13 weeks to transform 6 three-storey shop units into a pub on two floors which included a balcony overlooking a 30ft long bar. Victoria's (*right*) opened on 9th November 1987 but has since undergone a number of name changes – Strutt's, McCann's and now Bar Me (*below*).

Varsity, Green Terrace

This twenty-first century bar is located in the former University of Sunderland Galen Building. Its name reflects the premises former use.

White Hart, Queen Street

The White Hart (*left*) had been open over twenty years when it appeared on the 1857 map (*below*). This pub was another to go to make way for the inner ring road. Unfortunately no one informed the tenant, Frank Edward Pound, who found out the White Hart was to close and be demolished from a customer who had read it in the *Echo*.

Sons of the Wear, Queen Street

This bar dated from the 1830s and was probably named after Thomas Clarke's poem *Sons of the Wear*. The Licensing Sessions on 11th March 1959 agreed to the transfer of the licence from the Sons of the Wear to the Eagle at Pennywell.

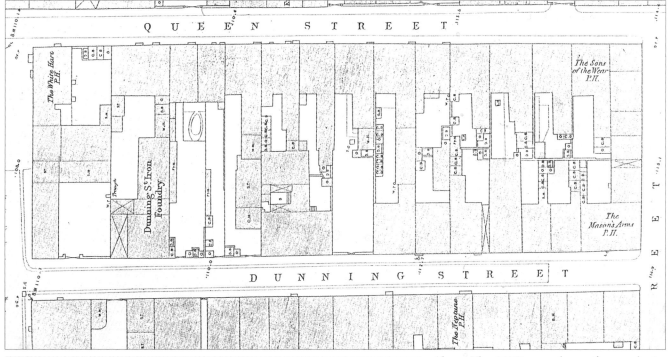

Above: The 1857 map shows four pubs in Dunning Street and Queen Street which have all now gone.

Masons Arms, Dunning Street

Formerly called the Borough Stores this pub was lucky to survive the Second World War when the opposite side of the road was destroyed in an air raid. The Masons was famous for its connection with betting. At one time bookies used to set out their stalls in front of the pub. Its last owner, Mr Oliver, was appropriately a racehorse and greyhound owner. It closed its doors for the last time on 1st October 1967 to make way for the inner ring road.

Oak Bar, South Street

This nineteenth century pub had a lucky escape in March 1943 during an air raid, although, William Jackson from the Oak Bar was taken to hospital with serious injuries. Three Fire Guards on duty in South Street were killed in the bombing. During the same raid two other pubs in town were hit. Parachute mines destroyed the Empress Hotel in Union Street and the Baltic Chambers in St Thomas Street. The Oak Bar closed in 1965 to make way for the inner ring road development.

The Neptune, Dunning Street

The Neptune (*above*) was known as the 'Number Nine' after its street number. In May 1897 the pub was raided by police for illegal betting. The landlord, John Lindsay, later appeared in court for using his licensed premises for betting. Tickets relating to horses running at Nottingham and Newmarket were found in the pub. He was found guilty and fined £25. The Number Nine had a name change in the 1970s to the Brewery Tap (*below*) after Vaux acquired the pub. The end of Vaux Brewery also saw the closure of the pub and then its demolition (*bottom*).

Cottage Tavern, Castle Street

When this beerhouse was offered for sale in 1882 it was described as having a bar, club room upstairs and a six-stalled stable in the yard. It closed on 16th March 1957.

Boulevard, High Street West

When Boulevard opened in the summer of 1980 it was Sunderland's only lager and wine bar. Under manager Jim Llewellyn it aimed to attract lunchtime trade from office workers, shoppers and shop-assistants. At night the target group was the 18-30s.

Harleys, High Street West

This bar opened in October 2001 in the building formerly occupied by the Woolwich Building Society. It is not named after Harley Street which lay behind the bar but after the Harley-Davidson motorcycle.

William Jameson, Fawcett Street
This J.D. Wetherspoon pub opened on 8th April 1997 in part of the old Binns department store. It was named after the man responsible for the layout of the Fawcett Street area in the 1800s.

Yates' Wine Lodge, Burdon House
Binns was just one of numerous owners of this building before it was converted into a bar in the 1980s. It started out as the Inn on the Park before becoming Blueberries. On 8th September 1994 it reopened as Rosie Malone's, being hailed as Sunderland's first Irish themed pub. After a £1 million makeover it opened as Yates' Wine Lodge in 1999.

Bar 36, Holmeside
This pub started life as the Wine Loft in 1978. Three years later it underwent a refurbishment giving it a thirties look and reopened as Marlowe's after the detective in Raymond Chandler's novels. It has since undergone another name change to Bar 36.

Sinatra's, Holmeside
Named after 'Old Blue Eyes' himself it opened on 10th December 1987. *Below*: An advert from 1881 for Digby Nelson's slate business which used to occupy the building. When Stan Nelson took over the Le Metro (Gannet) in High Street West his son Daryl became manager and he renamed the bar (*right*) after his great-grandfather. In 1966 the company supplied slates for the building of the Slipway at Town End Farm. After a period as the Funky Town the Holmeside pub has returned to Sinatra's.

DIGBY NELSON,
SLATER & SLATE MERCHANT,
Adjoining the Turkish Baths,
BOROUGH ROAD, SUNDERLAND.
———
Repairs promptly attended to.

The White Room, Holmeside
This bar was opened in August 2003 by three brothers – Ben, John and Rob Wall. The building used to house Josephs sports and toy shop.

Painted Wagon, Holmeside
Liberty's housed in part of the old Ritz Cinema building in 2003 when both lay derelict (*above*). The pub opened in 1974 as the Painted Wagon later becoming known as Traks. In 1989 the pub had a major makeover and reopened as Liberty's. The pub will open again when the redevelopment of the area is complete.

Berlins, Vine Place
This cafe bar was opened on 9th June 2002 by Peter Smith in the old premises of Fairman the chemists. It was named after songwriter Irving Berlin.

Luma, Derwent Street
This cafe bar and restaurant opened on 4th September 2003 in premises formerly occupied by Maurice Velody's shop.

Jazz, Vine Place
This bar opened as Mr Blue after the transfer of the licence from Fly McFly in Holmeside. It was taken over by Night Leisure and reopened on 9th July 2003 as Jazz.

Brogans, Crowtree Road
This bar opened on 12th February 1999 in the former Netto supermarket premises. It is named after Dave Brogan one of the four original partners.

ttonic, Vine Place
This bar and kitchen opened in May 2003 in the old Maxwells shop. Local businessmen Tony Griffiths and Eric Robson are ttonic's owners.

Chase, Park Lane
This late venue cafe bar opened in April 2002 in the former premises of Jonny Ringo's and Finos. Sam Krieger is the licensee of Chase.

Modo, High Street West
When this wine bar opened in 1988 *Dynasty* was one of the most popular series on television and the glamorous Carrington family gave the bar its name. In 1989 it reopened as Master's under Tony Smith (licensee) and Ray Howard (manager). Today the bar is called Modo (*above*).

SR1, High Street West
This bar is named after its post code. It was opened by Kevin Dobson in 2001 in the old Strothers hardware store.

Pravda, High Street West
This bar was formerly called the Lazi Pig but after a major makeover it was renamed Pravda. Owners Lazi Leisure also run Idols and Annabel's.

Idols, High Street West
Idols opened on 9th December 1987 and was modelled on Idols in Whitley Bay. Annabel's nightclub is housed in the upper floor of the building.

Rose and Crown, High Street West

This Bishopwearmouth pub dated back to the 1730s. Peggy Armour was licensee at the pub in the 1960s. In her pub career Peggy worked in the Hendon Gardens, the Chesters, the Wavendon and Grand Hotel. On occasions this pub did not serve exclusively alcohol as in the summer of 1964 when the Mayor J.R. Wilkinson had tea at the Rose and Crown with the Old Contemptibles (First World War veterans). In 1969 the Rose and Crown was demolished to make way for the inner ring road.

Star Inn, High Street West

In 1919 the Star Inn was reported to the Compensation Authority. When it closed the licensee was Tom McGowan and the owners Bewick and Charlton. The old beerhouse was formerly known as the Mariners Arms.

Coach and Horses, High Street West

In the early 1880s when George Edwards was innkeeper at the Coach and Horses it offered customers billiards, smoking rooms and good stabling for their horses. The Coach and Horses closed on Tuesday 29th September 1959 but manager, Bert Dawson, only found out from Newcastle Breweries it was closing the day before!

Tea Shop, High Street West

John Lavelle (on the right) behind the bar of the Tea Shop in the 1960s. It was known by this name because tea had at one time been sold from canisters behind the bar. From the 1860s the name officially recorded for these premises was Laing & Company. Until the early 1960s this bar and the Vestry in Fawcett Street were run together as a family business. An unusual feature of the pub in the old days were the tables and chairs which were made from barrels. In 1970 for the first time in over a century women were allowed in the bar. Under the name of the Scotch House it closed its doors for the last time in 1983.

Crown Inn, High Street West

The last manager in the Crown was local man Chris Sutherland (40) who had been in the pub for two years. Even before a closing date had been fixed the building was sold to a shoe retailers. Last orders were finally called at the Crown in 1960.

Crown and Thistle, High Street West

This pub, like many in High Street West, was handy for shoppers to pop in for a daytime drink. Like many of its neighbours it was served with a Compulsory Purchase Order and closed in 1966.

Three Crowns, High Street West

In the 1880s when Elizabeth Harley and her son were innkeepers at the Three Crowns it offered 'excellent accommodation for travellers' as well as good stabling. The pub closed in 1959 but the building still stands today. The last landlord, Watson Moralee (62), had been at the pub for 27 years. He described it as 'an institution more than a public house.' He recalled how it used to be packed every night during the last war with sailors from all over the world. He said 'I have had Americans in here who said they first heard of the Three Crowns in Jack Dempsey's bar in New York.'

Commercial Vaults, Green Street

This pub was known as the 'Long Bar' because it had the longest serving counter in Sunderland. The bar of this pub was gutted by fire on 16th January 1940. The cause of the blaze was not enemy bombs but a discarded cigarette. Fortunately the off-sales department, the upstairs buffet lounge, the storeroom, office and cellar escaped serious damage. It closed in 1968 as part of the town centre redevelopment scheme.

Bridge End Vaults, Matlock Street/Bridge Street

In May 1890 the Bridge End Vaults was undergoing major renovation when the building suddenly collapsed burying workmen under the rubble. Fortunately none were seriously injured. The pub was rebuilt and survived until 1967 when it was demolished to make way for the new inner ring road. Ann Thompson, landlady of the Bridge End Vaults when it closed said, 'It's sad to see the old place go, but trade has fallen off in recent years with changes in the area.'

Ann Thompson, landlady for the last dozen years of the Bridge End Vaults' life. In a 23 year career in the licensing trade Ann had also been in the Butchers Arms and Derby Hotel.

Bill Marshall (*below*) was one of Sunderland's best known publicans in the last century. Sunderland-born Bill learnt the pub trade as a barman at Wingate where he earned 18 shillings a week, of which 12 shillings went on his board. For this he worked from 6 in the morning until 11 at night. When he returned to Sunderland he took over as manager of the Central Hotel in Bridge Street. He then went on to run the Rowland Burdon Arms, Bridge Crescent;

Cottage Tavern, Castle Street; and the Crown, High Street West. Bill took over the tenancy of the Albion in 1934 which he was to run with his wife, Lilian, until his retirement in September 1966. One thing he refused to talk about was how he was awarded the Croix de Guerre in the First World War while serving with the 141st Heavy Battery Royal Garrison Artillery (Sunderland). The French honoured him for 'saving one man's life by his own gallant action and also saving his battalion's position.'

The Albion, Mary Street
After this beerhouse was reconstructed in the 1930s it was found many of its clientele wanted spirits to drink. Owners North-Eastern Breweries sacrificed one of its pubs to transfer a full licence to the Albion in April 1935. In 1983 after another refurbishment it reopened as Chaplins.

Phoenix Inn, Chester Road
This old pub had been going for seventy years when the 1901 Census was taken. At that time Usworth-born George Howey (29) was described as 'beer-retailer' at the Phoenix Inn. The pub can be seen in an aerial view of the area later in the century (*centre foreground where the road divides*). The Phoenix closed in the early 1970s as the area was redeveloped.

Substance, Tunstall Road
This lounge bar opened on 9th December 2001. Licensee Michael Wilds' motto for the bar is 'kick-back, relax and enjoy'. One of the features on offer at Substance is a heated patio.

The Licensing Magistrates annual meeting in 1940 revealed that Sunderland had 151 public houses, 68 beerhouses, 127 off-licences and 21 clubs. It was reported that since the Licensing Act had came into force in 1905 there had been 187 houses closed in that time. Compensation paid out amounted to £184,152 – an average of £936 a house. It was noted this was not from the public purse but from a compensation fund raised by taxation.

King Charlie & The Gannet TO The Little General & The Park Lane

Norfolk Hotel, Norfolk Street
The Norfolk Hotel opened in 1988 and three years later gained a pub licence. The building once housed the British Day School and it was here Sunderland and District Teachers' Association Football Club was formed which became Sunderland AFC.

BBs, St Thomas Street/West Sunniside
This bar was opened in 1987 by former Sunderland AFC director Barry Batey and named after his initials. It was located in the basement of the Maritime Building, the former Refuge Assurance Building (*left*).

The Gannet, High Street West
When Vaux and Associated Breweries opened the Gannet in 1969 it was described as a 'Dive Bar' as it was below street level and reached by a staircase. The Gannet being a bird famous for its diving ability. After being called the Le Metro, Digby's and Bar Mondo it is now known as the Underground.

Sunderland captain Charlie Hurley performed the opening ceremony at the Gannet on 23rd May 1969.

Olivers, Crowtree Road
The licence from BBs was transferred to Olivers (*left*). By coincidence a few doors along from BBs in Sunniside stood Blondies owned by Dave Brogan. Today Brogans stands next door to Olivers.

Sunderland's 1973 F.A. Cup-winning skipper, Bobby Kerr (*right*), went into the pub trade after ending his career. Today he runs the Copt Hill at Houghton having previously been at the Hastings Hill and Park Lane in Sunderland. When Bobby began in the Park Lane in 1987 he helped launch it with the help of

former team-mates Jimmy Montgomery, Jimmy McNab, Billy Hughes, Ron Guthrie, Mickey Horswill and Jeff Clarke.

Hastings Hill, Sevenoaks Drive
This pub opened in 1967 and was named after a nearby landmark. In March 1988 it had a £235,000 makeover which saw children's play areas and family dining facilities installed.

Park Lane, Park Lane
The Park Lane later changed its name to Bill Stickers but is now called Innfusion (*right*).

Star Hotel, Reynoldson Street

This pub was the scene of an unusual burglary on the night of 14th January 1907. Police found the intruder lying unconscious under the counter with a broken whisky bottle beside him. The man was still suffering the effects of drink when he appeared in court next day. The Star Hotel closed in 1972 after being open for over one hundred years.

The Chesters, Chester Road

This pub was converted from a vicarage in 1954 after plans to build a new hotel on the site had been rejected. In 2003 after 16 years at the Chesters publican Malcolm Essi and his wife Linden retired. Before the Chesters the couple had run the Smiths Arms, Shelter Deck, Double Maxim and Ivy House.

Ivy House, Worcester Terrace

The old Ivy House (*above*) which dated from the 1860s. At the Licensing Sessions in February 1940 the Smyrna Hotel's full licence was transferred to the Ivy House and plans were approved for alterations to the old pub.

The Royalty, Chester Road

This pub was formerly known as the Glebe Hotel. The name glebe related to church-owned land which occupied the site on which the original pub was built. In the 1890s Tom Dobson was the popular manager at the Glebe for seven years before taking up a post with James Deuchar wine and spirit merchants. In 1937 the owners sought to demolish and rebuild an enlarged pub. As the Corporation also wanted to widen Chester Road at the same time the Licensing Magistrates gave the scheme the go-ahead.

Fish Inn, Silksworth Row

Many Sunderland pubs did not survive the Depression of the 1930s and one of these was the Fish Inn in Silksworth Row. When Licensing Justices visited the pub on a Friday and Saturday night in 1935 there was not a soul in either night. Superintendent Cook reported 'The only time there is any business is when a party comes over from Gateshead to cheer the manager up.' It was also pointed out there were eight licensed houses within a radius of 190 yards of the Fish Inn. On 16th May 1935 the Fish Inn was one of three beerhouses the Licensing Justices 'extinguished' that day.

Museum Vaults, Silksworth Row

This nineteenth century beerhouse was formerly known as the Museum and Curiosity Vaults. It was one of the last pubs in Sunderland to serve only beer. On 12th January 1978 new tenant, Fred Wilson, successfully applied for a spirits and wine licence.

Black Swan, Silksworth Row
The original Black Swan stood in Hodgson's Buildings (*above*) and is seen on the 1857 map (*below*). This was later replaced with a new building known by locals as the 'Mucky Duck'. The pub closed in the 1970s but the building is still in use today.

Ship Isis, Silksworth Row
This pub started life as the Ship and it was the place where the crew members of a local ship called *The Isis* were always paid off. It became known by locals as the Ship Isis and the owners eventually renamed it that. Although the name change did not occur until after 1857 as it is shown on the map (*below*) as the Ship Tavern. In 1970 the

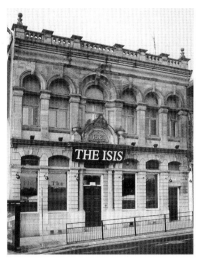

manager of the pub, Thomas Watson, received a gold watch for 40 years service with Scottish & Newcastle Breweries. He had been at the Ship Isis for 16 years having also worked in the Hendon Gardens, Palatine, the Crown, George and Dragon and Mountain Daisy. The present building dates from 1885. On 3rd April 1987 it reopened after a refurbishment as Livingstones (after the street in which the pub stands) under licensee Pat Henderson. For a time it was called Joe Bananas. In the summer of 2003 the pub reopened as the Isis with Denise Nicholson as landlady.

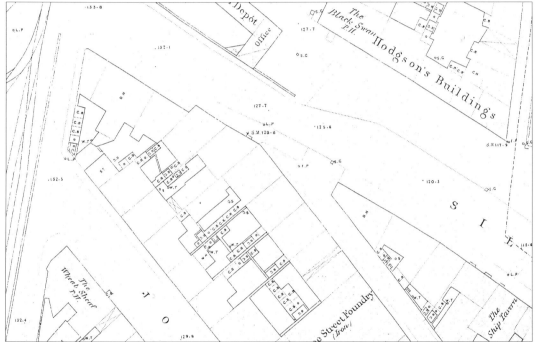

Wheat Sheaf Inn, Johnson Street
The Wheat Sheaf in Johnson Street shown on the 1857 map (*above*). When the pub was put up for sale in November 1873 it was described as being 'known for the last half century as a tavern doing excellent business'. This was helped by being close to a large glassworks, coal landsales and factories. The old Wheat Sheaf finally closed in 1958.

In his book *The Johnson Street Bullies* Patrick McLoughlin recalled an epic two hour fight which took place before the last war between his father, 'The Horseman', and a neighbour, 'Black Jackie'. In a scene reminiscent from *The Quiet Man* the protagonists even resembled the stars of the film – The Horseman was the image of John Wayne and Black Jackie the double of Victor McLaglen. The whole neighbourhood turned out to see the battle as it passed by the Temple Bar (known as the Bottom House) in South Johnson Street along to the Wheat Sheaf (the Top House) in Johnson Street. After being chased through a house Black Jackie slammed a door on his pursuer and knocked him out. His triumph was short-lived as The Horseman's wife, 'Gipsy Mary', knocked Black Jackie unconscious with a flat iron. With both men out cold the fight was declared a draw.

Temple Bar, South Johnson Street
Sunderland-born Dixon Howe (29) was innkeeper at this pub in 1901 where he lived with his family and servant. After one hundred years in business the Temple Bar closed in 1960.

King's Arms, Hanover Place

Ian Thompson (*below*), proprietor of the King's Arms from 1974 until 1989, recalled 'trade was great in the early days with shipyard lads at lunchtime and Pyrex lasses for basket meals. However, as we all know things changed by the '90s.' The owner and some of his regulars had a lucky escape on 5th March 1981 when a JCB digger ploughed into the pub. All escaped injury and the pub was open for business as usual after a few days.

The Saltgrass, Hanover Place

This pub took its name from this part of Deptford that had once been tidal wet land. It survives today only because its owners in 1944 failed to have its licence transferred to a proposed hotel on the site of the Chesters.

Shoulder of Mutton, Ropery Lane

For much of its life this pub lay in the shadow of Queen Alexandra Bridge as seen in this photograph. The old pub closed for the last time in 1960.

The Winston, Ayres Quay Road

Although only a licensed premises since the 1980s The Winston has its place in local history having been converted from a shipyard directors launch room.

The Ropery, Deptford Riverside

The old Webster's Ropery was converted into a pub in the 1980s and opened as Websters. Today it is called the Ropery.

Live and Let Live, Gerald Street

In 1935 the owners of the pub, North-Eastern Breweries, applied for the licence to be removed to the Albion (now Chaplins) in Mary Street. The Licensing Magistrates agreed although it was pointed out the owners were giving up the licence of a good house to get a full licence for the Albion.

Aylmer Arms, Aylmer Street

The Aylmer (*right*) was another Deptford pub to disappear in 1960. It had been open for over one hundred years.

Skiff Inn, Beach Street/Peacock Street

At one time rowing was a popular sport on the Wear and this pub took its name from a light sculling boat when it opened in the 1850s. After closing in the 1930s the building was used as a boys' club.

Free Gardeners Arms, Grafton Street/Enderby Road

In 1986 when Ron Robinson ran this bar he recalled how 'canboys' from the nearby Corning Glassworks called in for beer. Because of the nature of glassblowers' work they had been allowed a beer allowance dating back to the eighteenth century. They were carried in the enamelled cans with a hoop which were normally used by workmen for tea. One shift would send their canboy to the Free Gardeners while the other went to the Oddfellows Arms.

Sportsman's Arms, Deptford Road

This small beerhouse was put up for sale in June 1893 but was withdrawn after

bidding only reached £530. It eventually closed during the Second World War.

Black Cow, Ravensworth Street

This tiny bar, dating from the 1860s, still found room for a dartboard over the fire place. The old pub closed in 1976.

The Landsdowne, Deptford Road/Landsdowne Street

In 1878 when this pub was offered at auction one of its selling points was a very large upstairs room used for meetings of the several lodges held there. After changing its name to the Coopers Tavern it has now reverted back to its original name.

Earl Percy Arms, North Milburn Street

This pub started life in the early 1870s as the Earl Percy Arms named after the Earl of Northumberland. After more than 130 years in business the pub is still going strong under the name of the Cottage.

Westbury Arms, Westbury Street

In 1914 the Westbury Arms was one of half a dozen beerhouses run by James Wilson. Three were in nearby Trimdon Street: Engineers Arms, Glassmakers Arms and General Havelock. The others were the Museum Vaults in Silksworth Row and Earl Percy Arms in North Milburn Street. The Westbury Arms closed its doors for the last time in 1959.

Oddfellows Arms, North Ravensworth Street

This impressive looking pub is known by locals as Ted's after a former landlord Ted Elliott. This was one of a number of Oddfellows Arms in Sunderland. Oddfellowship on Wearside dates back to 1832 and from its earliest days there were strong ties with public houses. A number of early lodges began in pubs – Wear Mechanics Lodge at the Peacock Inn, High Street, in 1832 and Earl of Durham Lodge at the Black Swan, Silksworth Row, in 1838.

Caledonian Arms, Trimdon Street
The Caledonian Arms with the cooling tower of the Corporation's Electricity Generating Station in the background. The mid-nineteenth century pub closed in 1967.

Bus Inn, Trimdon Street
This pub dating from the 1860s was one of many that at one time stood in Trimdon Street. It closed in 1968 after trading for one hundred years.

General Havelock, Trimdon Street
The General Havelock lying derelict in the 1960s (*above*). It was one of three local pubs named after the Sunderland-born hero of the Indian Mutiny. This old beerhouse on the corner of Trimdon Street and Glass Street dated from the 1860s. In 1901 Buckinghamshire-born widow Sarah Maffey (43) is recorded as beerhouse-keeper at the General Havelock.

The Antelope, Trimdon Street West
When this pub was put up for sale in 1910 it was described as comprising large bar, family department and smoke-room on ground floor, five rooms on first floor, large cellar, warehouse and convenience in yard. This was another pub to close at the end of the 1960s.

Oddfellows Arms, Trimdon Street West
This pub was known to locals as Bouchers after former owners. The pub closed in 1958 after being open for over a century.

Bee Hive, Hylton Road/Milburn Street
In 1901 Scotsman David Elliott (41) was licensed victualler at this pub. In the 1960s the pub was called the Beefeater. Today under the name of Oddies, John and Pat Royal (*right*) run the pub. John was co-author of *Old Pubs of Sunderland*.

Railway Tavern, Westbury Street
This pub on the corner of Westbury Street and Hylton Road dates from the 1870s. On the night of the 1901 Census Sunderland-born John Booth (25) is recorded as barman at the pub where he lived with his family.

Crown and Sceptre, Hylton Road
When this pub was up for sale in 1889 it was advertised as having a 'frontage of 12 yards abutting on one of the leading thoroughfares of the town (Hylton Road)'. Sunderland-born Henry Christie was still publican at the pub in 1901 at the age of 67. In 1968 the Crown and Sceptre finally closed and was then demolished.

Jollies, Hylton Road
This pub opened in the 1990s beside where Millfield railway station stood. The Stonebridge, which opened shortly after it, stood opposite but was demolished to make way for the Metro.

Willow Pond, Hylton Road
In 1901 Scotsman John Wilson (38) was manager of this tavern. The pub is still going strong more than 130 years after first opening.

Mountain Daisy, Hylton Road
The imposing structure of the Mountain Daisy (*left*) is matched by its equally impressive interior. The original turn of the century glazed wall tiles and marble bar can still be seen in one of the ground floor rooms (*right*). In 1904 the pub could boast the 'most handsome and select billiard saloon in town (2 tables).' After a refurbishment in 1996 the pub reopened as Finnegan's Wake, one of Scottish & Newcastle Breweries' Irish concept pubs. The pub has now returned to its traditional name.

Pallion Inn, St Luke's Terrace
At the Licensing Sessions on 6th March 1936 North-Eastern Breweries successfully applied for the transfer of the licence from the Dog and Pheasant in Coronation Street to the Pallion Inn which was still in the planning stage. The brewery also surrendered the licences of the old Pallion Inn and the Skiff Inn at the same time. Today the pub provides a wide range of entertainment including quiz nights, pool tournaments and domino handicaps.

The Thorndale, Thorndale Road/Trent Road
When this Scottish & Newcastle Breweries' pub opened on 19th December 1966 the managers were Robert and Norah Stephenson. The couple had left the Dun Cow to take over the new pub. The nearby Thorney Close public house, which had opened the year before the Thorndale, is now demolished.

The Dolphin, Avonmouth Road/Ashdown Road
The Dolphin opened on 11th November 1960 and was run by Robert and Lilian Hedley with the help of their daughter Ann. The name was chosen by the chairman of Flowers Breweries who was a keen fisherman.

Round Robin, Hylton Road/Holborn Road
This pub opened in 1960 to serve the new housing estates which were built in the post-war era. In its early years the well known Eastender Jackie Dixon was compere at the Round Robin.

The Sandhill, Gleneagles Road
This pub was built on the site of the fifteenth century Grindon Old Hall and was named after a local landmark. It opened on 1st June 1965 under Robert and Lilian Hedley, the couple who had been the first managers of the Dolphin when it opened.

Prospect Hotel, Durham Road/Springwell Road
The Prospect Hotel was one of a new type of Sunderland pub when it was built in the 1930s. It was planned with motor vehicles in mind. Appropriately one of the pub's most memorable moments involved a motorcade – the return of the F.A. Cup in 1973 with some supporters standing precariously on the pub's roof (*right*).

Grindon Mill, Chester Road

On 2nd December 1891 the fully licensed Grindon Mill was put up for auction at the Queen's Hotel. It was part of the estate of Captain Beckwith going under the hammer which included 7 dairy farms, 15 cottages and the mansion Silksworth House. In the 1930s the Grindon Mill was rebuilt and now serves the large housing estates built in the post-war era. It has recently been taken over by Joe Foster and former Sunderland footballer Barry Dunn. Joe started out at the Welcome Tavern then ran the nightclubs Fosters and Close Encounters.

North Moor, Durham Road/North Moor Lane

This was another of the pubs built in the 1930s to serve the motorist and the westward expansion of housing estates. The pub changed its name in the 1970s to the Double Maxim. It closed and was demolished to make way for a McDonalds at the turn of the twenty-first century.

Ford Hotel, Hylton Road

The Ford Hotel was built in 1938 only after two South Hylton pubs (Commercial Hotel and Cambria Arms) were sacrificed by the owners. It closed in 1980 and after being targeted by vandals was demolished in May 1982.

Barnes Hotel, Durham Road

The Barnes Hotel continued the trend for pubs outside the town centre when it was built in the 1930s. The licence from the Oddfellows Arms in Barclay Street was transferred to the new hotel.

The Wavendon, Wavendon Crescent

The Wavendon opened on 7th August 1959. It took nine months to build at a cost of £30,000. The pub underwent a revamp in 1996 and was relaunched under the management of John and Dawn Robinson.

Jovial Friar, General Havelock Road

The Jovial Friar opened on 25th September 1963 under the management of husband and wife team Johnson and Joyce Hazard. The decor reflected the times with the wallpaper in the lounge described as 'aglow with brilliant turquoise, gold and black'. The Jovial Friar had been open less than forty years before it closed and was demolished.

The Eagle, Portsmouth Road/Parkhurst Road

This Nimmo house opened on 11th March 1959 claiming 'cool beer in a really clean glass is to be achieved at all times'. The materials used to build the pub included blue wall tiles from Sweden, Australian walnut panelling and Douglas fir from Canada for the walls. After lying derelict it became a target for arson attacks and was eventually demolished in October 1996.

Aquatic Arms, North Bridge Street

Sunderland wing half Arthur Housam (*right*) ran this pub in the 1950s after retiring from the game. He had just broken into Sunderland's first team when the Second World War put his playing career on hold. He was in the Sunderland side for the first F.A. Cup and League games after the war but was released by the club in 1948. The Aquatic closed in 1969 but its name lived on with a local football team (old regulars of the pub) bearing the name.

The Aquatic lying derelict (*above*) would have done a roaring trade on match days today.

Red Lion, Roker Avenue

A popular watering hole for supporters going to the Stadium of Light the Red Lion (*right*) was also packed on match days during the Roker Park years. Between 1983 and 1993 former professional footballer, Tony Smith, was licensee at the Red Lion. A skilful inside forward he was at West Ham in the days of Bobby Moore, Geoff Hurst and Martin Peters. After playing for Watford and Hartlepool, the PFA (the players' union) put him through a pub management training course and he later returned to his hometown to take over the Red Lion. Tony's brother, Jimmy, himself well known in local football circles, was bar manager at the 'Lion'. Another brother, Hughie, was one of Sunderland's most famous boxers and an Area lightweight champion.

Tony Smith in West Ham colours during the 1960s.

Colliery Tavern, Wayman Street

Now in the shadow of the Stadium of Light this pub is always packed on match days. In May 2003 the pub's much-loved landlady, Brenda Jones, lost her fight for life. She will be missed not only by Sunderland fans but supporters from all round the country who were made welcome there.

The Fort, Roker Avenue
This pub, dating from the 1850s, would have benefitted from match day trade even before Roker Park opened in 1898, as Sunderland played at nearby Newcastle Road before that. Today the Fort is one of the pubs that cater for fans going to the Stadium of Light.

Howard Arms, Roker Avenue
Licensee Scot Stewart (*left*) with son Craig, Keith Huslmeier and Phil Rouz on a match day at the Howard Arms in 1999. This pub dates from the 1870s and was formerly called the Burton House.

Wearmouth Bridge, Thomas Street
This pub was originally a three-storey building but in 1932 rebuilding plans were submitted to transform it into a single-storey premises. After a period as a restaurant it reopened as a pub in 1979 as the Terminus.

Jacksons, Dundas Street
This is another pub which is popular with supporters on match days. For years the Alexandra was known by locals as Jacksons after an owner between the wars. After a short period as the Benedict Biscop (founder of nearby St Peter's) it is now officially called Jacksons (*above*).

Cambridge Hotel, Fulwell Road
Former landlady of the Cambridge Hotel, Margaret Calvert (*right*), and barmaids ready to serve customers on route to Roker Park. Today the pub is run by Jan Holmes and Dave Colgin and supporters now call in on their way to the new ground.

Engineers' Tavern, Sheepfolds Road
This pub was known by locals as 'Ma Vick's' after one time landlady Elizabeth Ann Vickery. This pub was popular with pigeon men who had lofts on the nearby banks of the Wear.

Right: Mrs E.A. Vickery, first lady president of the Sunderland & District Licensed Victuallers Association. In 1949 when a report called for a reduction in the number of local pubs she said 'I have been in the public house business for 47 years and I hate to think that my little "dug-out" would be taken from me.'

The last licensee of the Engineers, Rose Roberts, seen behind the bar shortly before its closure in January 1971.

Grey Horse, Howard Street
A view of the Grey Horse shortly before its demolition in 1966. The pub had been closed since the Second World War and was finally cleared to make way for the building of multi-storey flats.

Colliery House, Brooke Street/Hay Street
This beerhouse took its name from nearby Wearmouth Colliery. A Compulsory Purchase Order forced its closure in 1962 and valued the pub at £1,750. Before she began at Ma Vick's, Rose Roberts was the last landlady of the Colliery House. Rose started working life as a welder at Steels and began working as a part-time barmaid at the Cambridge Hotel. In the early 1950s she took over the Colliery House.

Richmond Hotel, Hay Street
The house clearances in the Sheepfolds area in the early 1960s were the death sentence on pubs like the Richmond Hotel. The Compulsory Purchase Order valued the pub at £3,740 and it managed a brief stay of execution but finally closed on 17th June 1963.

Waggon Tavern, Brooke Street
This pub also owed its name to the local mining industry. Wagonways brought the coal to riverside staithes to be loaded on to boats. The pub's fate was sealed, along with that of the Richmond Hotel, at a Council Meeting in May 1962. Both had Compulsory Purchase Orders placed on them – the Waggon Tavern being valued at £2,700.

Oak Tree, North Bridge Street

This pub lay where the road sweeps round from Dame Dorothy Street on to the approach to Wearmouth Bridge. From 1959 to 1966 Elizabeth Steward ran the Oak Tree. She started pub work in the early '50s and when she left the Oak Tree she said 'During my 14 years I have learned one main thing: the Sunderland man likes good beer and if you can please him, then you can please anyone.' The old coaching inn closed in 1970.

Grapes Hotel, Dundas Street

This nineteenth century pub was built on the site of orchards and gardens. In 1901 William Cresswell (50) from North Shields was publican here. It survived when many of its neighbours closed but finally joined them in the 1980s.

Bee Hive Hotel, Liddell Street

In 1871 Peter McKey ran this pub when it was called the Liddell Street Tavern. It later became the Bee Hive and it was under this name that it closed in 1958. Jim Charlton, the proprietor in 1909 declared the Bee Hive provided the 'best drinks, pleasant company and popular landlord.'

Friendly Tavern, Yorke Street

This Scottish & Newcastle Breweries house served Barbary Coasters for over a century before finally closing its doors for the last time in 1958.

Olive Branch, Howick Street

This old pub started life in 1861 and closed as Monkwearmouth began to be redeveloped in 1959.

Pineapple Hotel, Charles Street/Liddell Terrace

This was another Scottish & Newcastle Breweries house that went in the redevelopment of the area in the 1950s and '60s. The Pineapple closed in 1958 after being open for a century.

Hope Tavern, Dixon Square

The night of 30th December 1933 was one of the more eventful occasions in the life of the Hope Tavern when it was raided by the police for after hours drinking. In court the following month P.C. Hutchinson reported the pub's landlord was still serving drinks at 10.18 pm (10 o'clock was last orders). The constable said when his back was turned one of the defendants drank off a full glass of beer. Three women who were found with full glasses on the table told the court they had not finished off because they had been talking. One man was accused of drinking stout on the night in question but said he had been drinking grapefruit. He said 'I never drink stout because it's too expensive'. When a glass containing beer was produced as

evidence one of the accused said it seemed fresher than on the night of the raid. All the defendants were found guilty. The licensee was fined £2 for selling intoxicating liquor during non-permitted hours and his wife was fined £1 for aiding and abetting. Fourteen of the pub's locals were each fined five shillings. The Hope Tavern closed its doors for the last time in November 1960.

Borough Hotel, Yorke Street

In 1891 this pub was advertised as having a 'large front sitting bar, front sitting room and back bar snug.' The snug was a place where women could go for a chat and a drink away from men. On 11th March 1959 the Licensing Justices agreed to the transfer of the licence of the Borough to the Pennywell.

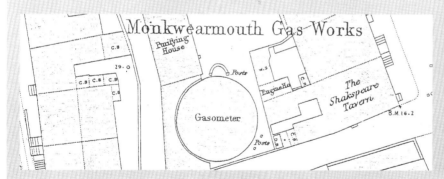

Shakespeare Tavern, Strand Street

The Shakespeare Tavern seen on the 1857 map standing beside the local gasworks near Folly End. In 1901 Shildon-born William Young (46) was recorded as licence victualler at the Shakespeare Tavern. The old tavern was to remain open only another half dozen years before its closure.

Shipwrights Arms, Dame Dorothy Street

This pub was affectionately known by locals as the 'Duzzy House'. This probably relates to the strength of beer served there which made drinkers dizzy (duzzy). The Shipwrights Arms early in the last century (*left*) and shortly before its closure in 1962 (*above*).

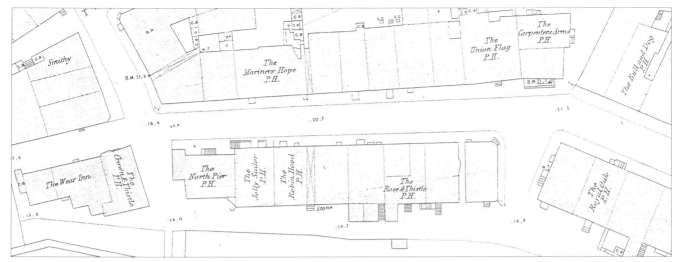

Above: The 1857 map of the Monkwearmouth riverside shows the area almost rivalled the East End for pubs. Almost all of these pubs around Wear Street and North Quay were closed within a few years of the map's publication.

Bonner's Field, Bonner's Field

The large bonded warehouse that stood on the Monkwearmouth riverside was transformed into a pub in 1982 and was named the Bonner's Field (*right*) after its location. After a fire caused extensive damage the building was renovated and renamed St Peter's Wharf. It was later called Planet Football but closed and now forms part of a luxury flats complex.

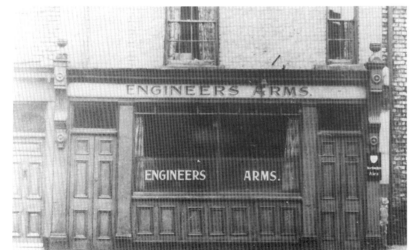

Engineers Arms, Whickham Street

The Engineers Arms (*left*) was one of four Sunderland pubs raided on the afternoon of 17th May 1905 for illegal betting. Everyone in the pub at the time was taken to the police station to be questioned and books and papers were seized. The next day the Engineers' landlord, Joseph Stephenson, appeared in court charged with keeping licensed premises for the purpose of betting. He was found guilty and fined £10 and costs. Half a dozen men who were in the pub at the time of the raid were charged with 'resorting to the Engineers Arms for the purpose of betting' but had their cases dismissed. The pub finally closed in 1963.

Williamson Arms, Church Street

One of the attractions of the Williamson Arms (*right*) was having its own quoit ground at the back of the premises. (At one time this was a very popular pastime with men of the region.) The pub was named after the famous family who at one time owned virtually all of Monkwearmouth. It did not survive the Depression and closed in 1933.

Clipper Ship, Victor Street

This pub opened in the middle of the nineteenth century and was named after the clipper ships built in the Wear shipyards. Right up to its closure in 1962 the bar was popular with shipyard workers from the nearby North Sands Yard.

Jack Crawford, Whitburn Street/Charles Street

This nineteenth century pub, named after the Sunderland-born 'Hero of Camperdown', met its end in an air raid during the Second World War. The figure of Crawford climbing the mast to nail back the colours back can be seen on the corner of the pub.

Victor Hotel, Victor Street

The Victor Hotel in the 1960s shortly before its demolition (*below*). This pub was so small the dartboard was behind the bar and the doors had to be locked during a darts match. Its life might have been shorter still if its owner in 1898 had got his way. Jack Clough wanted to give up the licence in exchange for a full licence for another pub.

New Clipper, Zetland Street/Whickham Street

This pub was built in the 1960s at a time when the trend in the area was for pub closures. It stands on the site of Ernst Lautebach's Mineral Water Works. In 1968 Sunderland Supporters' Club took over the pub as its headquarters but later returned to being an ordinary pub again. Over the years it has had a number of variations on its name – Clipper Ship (*above*), the Clipper and now the New Clipper.

The Albion, Dock Street/Victor Street

On the afternoon of 8th May 1907 the Albion's barman, James Knox, was cleaning spittoons in the yard of the pub when he was struck by lightning. He had to be carried inside and then taken to Monkwearmouth Hospital for rest and recuperation. *Above right*: Two Barbary Coasters outside the Albion during the war years – John Solomon (right) and Bill Wyness.

Barrington Hotel, Barrington Street/Millum Terrace
In the days when betting was illegal the back lane of
Barrington Street was used by bookies to take bets.
Lookouts were placed at either end of the lane to warn
of approaching police. The Barrington closed in 1961.

Vulcan Hotel, Millum Terrace
In February 1938 the Vulcan Hotel was one of three
Newcastle Breweries' houses which police sought to
close. They reported to the Brewster Sessions that there
were eight licensed premises within 300 yards of the
Vulcan Hotel. The brewery said they were prepared to
give up two of the houses, the George IV in Hanover
Place and the Hedworth Hotel in Hedworth Street, if the
Vulcan remained open. The brewery said they would not

be prepared
to spend
money on
improvements
to the Vulcan
if they did not
think it was a
good house.
The Justices
agreed and
the Vulcan
Hotel was to
remain open
for another 25
years.

William Pile, Dame Dorothy Street
This pub was named after one of Sunderland's most
famous shipbuilders of the nineteenth century. His
shipyard at North Sands built both wooden and iron
vessels. The pub bearing his name was one of the first to
go in the redevelopment of the area in 1959.

Princess of Wales, Hardwicke Street
Children on the steps of the Princess of Wales. At one
time this was a common sight at closing time with
youngsters looking for spare coppers from drinkers.
The pub closed in 1963 just short of a century since its
opening.

Marquis of Lorne, Zetland Street
This beerhouse on the corner of Millum Terrace and
Zetland Street was put up for auction in July 1920. It
comprised a bar and two sitting rooms on the ground
floor, three rooms on the first floor, large yard, cellar
and 'up-to-date sanitary arrangements'. The Marquis of
Lorne was popular with shipyard workers and in the
1960s the landlady kept a slate for regulars. However, if
they did not settle up on pay day and deliberately
avoided the landlady their names were displayed in the
bar for all to see. The shipyards were still in their
heyday when the pub closed in 1965.

Pear Tree, Hardwicke Street
The Pear Tree beerhouse in Hardwicke Street was
known by locals as the Old Boat. In 1932 the police
objected to the renewal of the licence of the pub on
the grounds it was surplus to requirements.
Superintendent Cook told the Licensing Magistrates
that the police had kept watch on the premises. He
said 'we were there about half-an-hour, and no one
came in except a kiddie to ask the time.' It was
revealed the takings of the Pear Tree were £25 a
week of which £2 15 shillings was paid to the
landlord and his wife. Despite the police objections
the Magistrates decided to renew the licence –
delaying last orders at the Old Boat for another
thirty years or so.

Charlie & The Wheat Sheaf TO Warney & The Sheet Anchor

Charles Thomson (*right*), Sunderland and Scotland captain before the First World War, went into pub management in the 1920s. The hard tackling centre-half signed from Hearts in 1908. It took £700 to lure him south of the border. At the time there was a transfer limit of £350 and the difference was made up by a make-weight player. The highlight of his Roker career came in the 1912-13 season when he almost helped Sunderland to the 'Double'. He led the side in the F.A. Cup Final at Crystal Palace before a huge crowd of over 120,000. They went down to a 1-0 defeat to Aston Villa then showed great character a few days later by drawing at Villa Park to virtually clinch the championship. He went into the Forces during the First World War and did not resume his playing career after the war ended but became a pub manager in Scotland. He returned to Sunderland and was running the Wheat Sheaf in the early 1930s. He also helped out at the nearby Blue Bell in Roker Avenue and the Royal Hotel in North Bridge Street. He died in a nursing home in Edinburgh on 6th February 1936 but his funeral was on Wearside with hundreds paying their last respects to the popular Sunderland and Scotland skipper at Mere Knolls Cemetery. A card on one of the floral tributes read, 'In memory of a dear friend from the staffs and customers of the Wheat Sheaf Hotel, Royal Hotel and Blue Bell Hotel.'

Wheat Sheaf Hotel, Thomas Street/ Roker Avenue

In its early days the Wheat Sheaf was an important coaching inn. In 1827 the horse-drawn coach 'Lion' left from here every morning at 10 o'clock bound for South Shields, returning at 5 pm. By 1834 there was a gig leaving for Shields nearly every hour. The Wheat Sheaf was also a place farm hands met farmers for hirings. In 1997 the upper floors of the pub were converted into student flats.

Royal Hotel, North Bridge Street

When Monkwearmouth Railway Station opened in 1848 the architect, Thomas Moore, drew up plans for the neighbouring Royal Hotel. The hotel had a lucky escape during an air raid on 9th August 1940 when a bomb landed on the nearby rail bridge across Sheepfolds Road. The only damage the hotel sustained was broken windows. The Royal Hotel closed in 1967 and is seen lying derelict (*right*) before it was knocked down.

Blue Bell, Roker Avenue

This pub dated back to the days when Roker Avenue was known as Broad Street. It was rebuilt in 1900 and was an impressive part of the Monkwearmouth landscape until the night of 7th November 1941 when it was wrecked in an air raid (*below*). Although permission was granted to rebuild the Blue Bell it never went ahead.

Sheet Anchor, Dundas Street

Former Sunderland and England full back, Warneford 'Warney' Cresswell (*below*), was landlord at the Sheet Anchor for a period in the 1940s and '50s. He was already an England international when Sunderland paid South Shields a record £5,500 fee for his services in 1922. He won further caps at Roker Park before moving on to Everton in 1927. After Warney's playing days were over he tried his hand at

football management before becoming a licensee after the war. Warney's son Corbett spent part of his childhood at the Sheet Anchor. Like his father, Corbett also had a distinguished football career. Although he had a brief spell in League football with Carlisle he made his name in the amateur game. An outstanding centre-half with the all-conquering Bishop Auckland side of the '50s Corbett was also an England Amateur international. After more than 120 years in business the Sheet Anchor closed in 1965.

Derby Hotel, Millum Terrace
When this pub was put up for sale in 1890 it was advertised as having a bar, front and back snugs, two sitting rooms, bottling cellar, washrooms and a large cemented yard. Also included was a private apartment of four large rooms. The property was bought for £2,725. The Derby closed in 1962 and was demolished for the Corporation flat development scheme.

New Derby, Roker Baths Road
When the New Derby opened on 4th September 1963 the interior was designed to reflect a Scandinavian atmosphere with the use of stone and timber. The first manager in this Nimmo's house was Stephen Stronach who ran it with the help of his wife Rose.

Lanercost, Harbour View
In 1976 Ron Dodd and his wife Sandra converted their hotel and restaurant into a pub. After successfully applying for a public house licence there followed a long legal battle with the Council which dragged on for years. In 1984 two Wear pilots, Ian Swann and Duncan Callander, took over the pub and changed its name to the Pilot Cutter (*right*). Today the pub is called the Harbour View.

Wolseley Hotel, Millum Terrace
This pub was named after Field Marshal Garnet Wolseley who, in an Army career of half a century, served in the Crimean War, Indian Mutiny, Chinese War and was Commander-in-Chief in the Boer War. Sunderland-born William Forrester (27) was bar manager at the Wolseley in 1901 and the pub is still going strong a century later.

The Cliff, Mere Knolls Road
This Scottish & Newcastle Breweries' house opened on 2nd November 1966 with Elizabeth Steward as manageress and licensee. With Roker Park nearby it was always popular with supporters on match day. The football ground has gone but the pub is still going strong.

Queen Vic, Harbour View
This pub opened in 1997 in what had been the Roker Victory Club. Another pub with an *Eastenders* television series connection in its name.

Roker Hotel, Roker Terrace

In 1902 this hotel was claiming Roker as the 'Brighton of the North'. In the 1840s, as the Roker Baths Hotel, it was offering full board or bed and breakfast to guests, a variety of baths (warm, cold or vapour) and 'use of sea bathing machine, 3d; if taken into the sea with a horse, 6d.' After more than a century and a half it is still one of the most popular hotels for locals and visitors alike.

Puffin' Billy, Whitburn Road

This pub opened at Seaburn on 6th July 1989. The £1 million development included restored Pullman railway carriages. *Puffing Billy* was the world's first locomotive (predating George Stephenson's *Rocket*). It is now known as the Pullman Lodge.

Smugglers, Lower Promenade

On 29th May 1986 Nelsons opened in the renovated building which formerly housed the Ro-Ko-Ko night club. The pub, run today by Donna Gibson, could not be closer to Roker Beach (*above*).

La Fontaine, Queen's Parade

In 1976 this former restaurant reopened as the Saxon Hotel under manageress Margaret Short. Three years later it was renamed the Henry VIII. In 1989 more than £90,000 was spent on renovating the shell of the Henry VIII. The pub reopened under Dave and Pat Henderson as La Fontaine.

Seaburn Hotel, Queen's Parade

Built at a cost of £20,000 in the 1930s the Seaburn Hotel took only fourteen weeks to complete. In recent years it has undergone major refurbishment under the name Swallow Hotel and now the Marriott.

Bay Hotel, Whitburn Bents Road

The old Bay Hotel around 1960 (*right*) when dances were a popular attraction. In the 1960s and '70s the Bay was a regularly venue for rock groups. The Who, Pink Floyd, Free and Tyrannosaurus Rex (later T Rex) all appeared at the Bay. After being found structurally unsafe the old Bay had to be demolished and was replaced by a new £1 million building in the mid '80s. Amazingly the replacement building was itself pulled down in 2003 to make way for flats.

Grange Hotel, Newcastle Road/Thompson Road
When the Grange Hotel was opened in the 1930s it was one of the new wave of pubs built with the motor car in mind. Its location on the main route to Newcastle sought to attract passing traffic. The area was not as built up as it is today but the residents who were there campaigned against its opening. At the Magistrates meeting on 4th April 1935 to confirm the removal of the licence from the Cyprus Hotel in Church Lane to the Grange Hotel there were protests from locals. They claimed the pub already had an effect on house prices in the area, reducing new houses being built by £70 each. Despite the objections the pub got its licence and flourishes to this day.

Sunderland Flying Boat, Sea Road
When the Salutation Inn in Hendon closed in 1957 the license was transferred to a new pub to be built on Sea Road. This was to bear the same name but when it opened just before Christmas 1959 it was named the Royal Marine. In 1987 after the pub was given a £240,000 face lift it reopened as the Sunderland Flying Boat.

Windmills, Station Road
This pub opened on 27th March 1987 on the site of an old garage. Run by Ann Veti and her brother Walter, Windmills (Fulwell Mill is a short distance away) was described as a pub, wine and diner. It provided a video wine bar, traditional bar room, restaurant facilities and children's play area.

Millers Inn, Fulwell Quarry
Built next to the golf centre at Fulwell Quarry, the Fairway, opened on 20th November 1996. Today this family pub is called Millers Inn.

Taylor's, Dovedale Road/Alston Crescent
The Lane Arms opened just before Christmas 1965 having stood empty after its completion until being taken over by William Jackson. The first manager was Denis Rogers (41) who had been bar manager at the Grand Hotel for ten years. He had followed his father, Walter, into the pub trade. Walter had been manager at the Neptune in Dunning Street and the Wellington Inn at Stoney Lane. The Dene Estate pub is now called Taylor's after the owner.

Blue Bell, Fulwell Road
The present Blue Bell dates from the early 1930s when it was built alongside the old premises to maintain continuity of the licence. The building demolished in 1932 had itself replaced an earlier Blue Bell which had catered for the small village of Fulwell from the 1820s.

Old Mill, Southwick Green

Both the Old Mill and the Smiths Arms, which stood only a few yards away, dated from the 1820s. Jane Wilkinson (29) from Newcastle was innkeeper at the Old Mill in 1901. She lived there with her husband, Nathan, family and two servant girls. The Old Mill and the Smiths Arms were both demolished in the 1980s.

Smiths Arms, Southwick Green

A blacksmith's stood next to this pub hence the name. William Kirton (43) from Willington Quay was innkeeper (manager) at the Smiths Arms in 1901. He lived there with his Yarmouth-born wife Ellen (45). They had their first son at Willington Quay then a daughter and three more sons at Southwick.

Albion Hotel, Southwick Road

The Albion Hotel (*left*) is known by locals as the Bush. The pub dates from the early 1870s and is still going strong today. It has benefitted in recent years with the building of the Stadium of Light nearby.

Mill House Inn, Southwick Road

In 1901 the Mill House Inn stood next to seven miners' homes called 'Halfway House' – the pub's present name. At this time Matthew Cuthbertson Robson (31) from Philadelphia, County Durham, was manager at the Mill House Inn. He lived there with his wife Eliza from Chatham, Kent, three sons and a local girl working as a domestic servant. In May 1973 landlord, John Brian Armstrong, had the Halfway House painted in red and white stripes in honour of Sunderland's historic F.A. Cup victory.

Sun Inn, Southwick Green

When this pub was put up for sale in May 1889 the advert said 'great and important additions have recently been made and is now the most extensive, commodious and best business hotel in the neighbourhood.' The pub changed hands for £6,500.

Tram Car Inn, Southwick Green

In 1901 Sunderland-born George W. Clark (24) was publican at the Tram Car Inn. He was married to a Southwick girl, Lizzie, and had two small children at the time of the Census. Landlord today is Louis Morgan who runs the pub with wife Kate.

Friendly Tavern, Southwick Road

The Friendly Tavern (*left*), dating from the 1850s, stood near the Halfway House. At the 1962 Brewster Sessions the transfer of the licence from Margaret Armstrong of the Friendly Tavern to her son John Armstrong was approved. It remained open only a few more years and was then demolished.

The Station, Stoney Lane
Standing at the bottom of Stoney Lane the Station was known by locals as Tates after a nineteenth century licensee William Tate. The Station closed in 1968 on the same day as two other Southwick pubs – The Alexandra and Wellington Inn.

The Alexandra, Clockwell Street
When this pub was pub up for sale in November 1876 it comprised a bar, front sitting room, back sitting room, three rooms upstairs as well as yard, washhouse and outhouses.

Wellington Inn, Wellington Street
In the 1901 Census Southwick-born Michael Oliver (42) is recorded as bottlemaker and publican at the Wellington Inn. He lived there with his wife, Elizabeth, who was from South Shields, and two daughters and five sons (the eldest of whom was a barman).

Pedestrian Arms, Victoria Street
Licensee Thomas Clark and wife Elizabeth outside the Pedestrian Arms. The couple ran this beerhouse from the First World War until its closure in 1930. The Pedestrian Arms was one of 25 pubs in Southwick at the time of its incorporation into Sunderland in 1928. This meant that the area's pubs now came under the jurisdiction of Sunderland Licensing Magistrates. One of the consequences of this was that eight (almost a third of Southwick pubs) closed by 1939.

Banks of the Wear, King Street
The original Banks of the Wear dated from the middle of the nineteenth century but was rebuilt in 1909 and served the residents of Low Southwick until its closure in 1964.

Right: Mary Price at the back of the Banks of the Wear. She was the pub's landlady from 1906 until her death in 1948 at the age of 68.

Cricketers Arms, Pilgrim Street

Dating from the 1870s this pub served locals for over one hundred years. It was closed in 1976 to make way for redevelopment of the Pilgrim Street area. At one time along Pilgrim Street from the Cricketers stood the Neptune Tavern. In 1885 it was claiming to sell the best ale in the County at 1d, 1$\frac{1}{2}$d, 2d, 2$\frac{1}{2}$d, and 3d a glass. The quality of its beer could not save the Neptune and it closed in 1936.

North Star, Kings Road

In the late 1950s and '60s James Foster was licensee at the North Star. After working for a brewery for 12 years he decided to go into the licensing trade. After a refurbishment in 1981 the North Star was renamed the Sheltered Deck after the SD14 cargo ships built at the nearby shipyards. However, after it was pointed out SD stood for Shelter Deck the name was changed the following year. The pub has now reverted to its original name.

West Country Arms, Ogle Terrace

This pub began serving customers in the 1860s. Shortly before the Second World War it closed. At one time there were two pubs of the same name in the East End.

General Havelock, Stoney Lane

Tom Worthy (51) publican at the pub in 1901 was a local man but his wife, Maria, was from King's Lynn in Norfolk. The Hogan family ran the General Havelock from the First World War until 1977 when Nancy McVay (née Hogan) retired. Not surprisingly it became known to locals as Hogan's and now it is officially called that.

Times Inn, Wear Street

Locals, bar staff and passers-by outside the Times Inn at the turn of the twentieth century when James Wakinshaw was landlord. After closing as a pub after the First World War the building was put to various uses. The neighbouring Pickersgill shipyard eventually acquired the premises and used it as a store. After standing derelict for a number of years the old Times Inn was rebuilt and opened for business under its original name in 1986.

Dray and Horses, Thompson Road
The first pint at the Dray and Horses was drawn by Mayor Mary Miller on Guy Fawkes' Day 1969. Appropriately the beer was delivered from Vaux Brewery by two drays pulled by Percheron horses.

The Wearsider, Emsworth Road
Carley Hill had to wait until 1972 before it got its own pub with the opening of the Wearsider.

The Wessington, Wessington Way
This family pub opened on 8th October 1993 with Paul and Pauline Greaves the licensees. Wessington was the old name for Washington.

Cauld Lad, Cockermouth Road/Caithness Road
This Scottish & Newcastle Breweries' pub opened a week before Christmas 1963. Chris Sutherland first ran the pub which was named after the old ghost legend at Hylton Castle.

The Slipway, Blackwood Road
Nellie Stevenson was the first manageress at the Slipway when it opened on 6th December 1966. It was designed with a shipyard feel with the bar made to represent the riveted steel plates of a ship.

The Torrens, North Hylton Road
Named after the famous Sunderland-built ship, the Torrens opened on 6th September 1967. It was a favourite with Plessey workers before the factory, which stood over the road to the pub, closed.

The Dagmar, Wembley Road
Formerly the Thistle Club, when it was converted into a pub in 1987 it was renamed after the pub in the *Eastenders* television series.

Quincey's, Timber Beach Road
This roadside pub just off Wessington Way opened its doors for the first time in 1997.

Castletown Inn, Castle View
The Castletown Inn opened in 1879 when its customers would have been furnacemen and ironworkers from the nearby Wear Rolling Mills. In the 1990s it was known as the Crown and Anchor. Today the premises is a furniture shop.

The Schooner, Berwick Avenue
The Schooner was opened on 23rd November 1966 under the management of Henry Nutter and his wife Elizabeth. The pub was less than thirty years old when it was closed and knocked down.

Monty & The Duck TO The Red & White Arms

The Duck and Kangaroo, Ravenswood Road
When this Vaux pub was opened by Sunderland goalkeeper Jimmy Montgomery on 2nd July 1969 it was described as a mixture of Victorian and modern (psychedelic). It was named after a poem by Edward Lear. It was later renamed the Phoenix and then Toddy's (*above*).

Left: Jimmy Montgomery – one of Sunderland's greatest keepers of all-time. The pinnacle of his career was the brilliant double save at Wembley in 1973 which ensured the Cup came back to Wearside for the first time since Raich Carter & Co in 1937.

Mickey Horswill (*right*), a member of Sunderland's 1973 F.A. Cup-winning side, went into pub management after retiring from the game. At one time he ran the Shipwrights Arms at Red House.

Shipwrights Arms, Rotherfield Road
The Shipwrights Arms was the first pub on Red House Estate when it opened on 19th November 1963. The new Truman house was run by Douglas and Elizabeth Walton with the help of barmaids Catherine Coates and Doreen Bolden.

Stephen and Rose Stronach ran the Dray and Horses (*above*) when it first opened. Their son Peter (*right*) went on to play for Sunderland AFC. He was outstanding for England Schoolboys making eight appearances for his country. He signed as an apprentice at Roker Park in 1972 and went on to make his League debut for the club.

Hylton Castle Arms, Canterbury Road
The 'Arms' was painted with red and white stripes in 1992 when Sunderland reached the F.A. Cup Final. It was the local of Sunderland footballers David Rush and Kieron Brady. This was the first pub on Hylton Castle Estate when it opened in 1959.

Index of Pubs

Liberty's, Holmeside 36
Liddell Street Tavern, Liddell Street/Barclay Street 53
Linden Arms, Linden Place 17
Live and Let Live, Gerald Street 44
Livingstones, Silksworth Row 43
Londonderry Hotel, High Street West 29
Londonderry Hotel, Surtees Street 16-17
Lord Nelson, Nile Street 24
Lord Roberts, Winchester Terrace 16
Luma, Derwent Street 37

McCanns, Low Row 33
Mackem Bar, Hendon Road 15
Maggie May's, Holmeside 30
Maple Bar, Ford Street 18
Mariner's Arms, High Street West 38
Mariner's Hope, Wear Street 55
Mariners Tavern, Low Street 13
Market Hotel, Coronation Street 8
Marlowe's, Holmeside 36
Marquis of Lorne, Millum Terrace 57
Marriott Hotel, Queen's Parade 60
Masons Arms, Dunning Street 34
Masons Arms, Low Street 4
Master's, High Street West 37
Meux's Arms, Coronation Street 8
Mill House Inn, Southwick Road 62
Modo, High Street West 37
Monkwearmouth Colliery, Low Quay 10
Mountain Daisy, Hylton Road 43, 47
Mowbray Arms, Borough Road 27
Mowbray Park Hotel, Borough Road 27
Mr Blue, Vine Place 37
Mr Smith's, Bedford Street 21
Museum Vaults, Silksworth Row 42, 45

Nelson's, Lower Promenade 60
Neptune, Dunning Street 34-35, 61
Neptune Tavern, Pilgrim Street 64
New Bridge, Lombard Street 8
New City, Holmeside 30
New Clipper, Zetland Street/Whickham Street 56
New Derby, Roker Baths Road 59
New Shades, Hendon Road 14
Norfolk Hotel, Norfolk Street 41
Norfolk House (Hotel), Norfolk Street 24
North Moor, Durham Road/North Moor Lane 49
North Pier, North Quay 55
North Star, Kings Road 64
Nutwith Hotel, Coronation Street 8-9

Oak Bar, South Street 35
Oak Tavern, Silver Street 10
Oak Tree, North Bridge Street 53
Ocean Queen, Tower Street 23
Oddfellows Arms, Barclay Street 49
Oddfellows Arms, Church Street 26
Oddfellows Arms, North Ravensworth Street 45
Oddfellows Arms, Fowler Street 23
Oddfellows Arms, Trimdon Street West 46
Oddies, Hylton Road 46
Old Mill, Southwick Green 22, 62
Old Twenty Nine, High Street West 29
Old Vestry, Fawcett Street 27
Olive Branch, Howick Street 53
Olivers, Crowtree Road 41
Outpost, High Street West 28
Oxford Hotel, High Street East 6

Painted Wagon, Holmeside 36
Palatine Hotel, Toward Road 27, 43
Pallion Inn, Lister Street
Pallion Inn, St Luke's Road 48
Parade Hotel, Hendon Parade 16
Park Inn, Olive Street 30
Park Lane, Park Lane 41
Paul Pry, Silver Street 10
Peacock Inn, High Street West 29, 45
Pear Tree, Hardwicke Street 57
Pedestrian Arms, Victoria Street 63
Phoenix, Ravenswood Road 13, 66
Phoenix Inn, Chester Road 40
Pilot Cutter, Harbour View 59
Pineapple Hotel, Charles Street 53
Planet Football, Bonner's Field 55
Plough Inn, Low Row 32
Polly's, Lambton Street 12
Porcupine Park, Queen Alexandra Road 19
Post Office Restaurant, Nile Street 24
Pravda, High Street West 37
Prince of Wales, Hill Street 17

Princess of Wales, Hardwicke Street 57
Prospect Hotel, Durham Road/Springwell Road 48
Puffin' Billy, Whitburn Road 60
Pullman Lodge, Whitburn Road 60

Quavers, Lambton Street 21
Quayside Exchange, High Street East 3
Queen Vic, Harbour View 59
Queen's Head, Low Row 32
Queen's Hotel, Fawcett Street 22
Queen's Hotel, Hendon Road 14
Quincey's, Timber Beach Road 65

Railway Tavern, Low Quay 10
Railway Tavern, Westbury Street 47
Red Lion, Crowtree Road 28
Red Lion, Roker Avenue 50
Refreshment Rooms, Sunderland Railway Station 31
Regale Tavern, East Hendon Road 11
Richmond Hotel, Hay Street 52
Riggers Arms, High Street East 10
Rink Hotel, Hudson Road 20
Rising Sun, Trimdon Street 23
Robert Burns Arms, Coronation Street 8-9
Robin Hood, High Street East 4, 10
Robin Hood, North Quay 55
Roker Hotel, Roker Terrace 60
Ropery, Deptford Riverside 44
Rose and Crown, Bedford Street 21
Rose and Crown, High Street West 38
Rose and Thistle, North Quay 55
Rosedene, Queen Alexandra Road 19
Rosie's Bar, High Street West 29
Rosie Malone's, Burdon Road 36
Round Robin, Holborn Road/Hylton Road 48
Rovers Return, Ward Street 17
Rowland Burdon Arms, Bridge Crescent 25, 40
Royal Hotel, North Bridge Street 58
Royal Hotel, Prospect Row 7
Royal Marine, Sea Road 14, 61
Royal Oak, North Quay 55
Royal Standard, High Street East 5
Royal Tent, High Street West 29
Royalty, Chester Road 42

Saddle Inn, High Street East 6
Salem Hotel, Salem Street 20
Saltgrass, Hanover Place 44
Salutation Inn, Hendon Road 14, 61
Sandcastle, Ryhope Road 19
Sandhill, Gleneagles Road 48
Savannah, Holmeside 30
Saxon Hotel, Queen's Parade 60
Schooner, Berwick Avenue 65
Scotch House, High Street West 38
Scott's, High Street West 28
Seaburn Hotel, Queen's Parade 60
Shakespeare Tavern, Strand Street 54
Sheet Anchor, Dundas Street 58
Shelter Deck, Kings Road 42, 64
Ship Inn, High Street East (No. 1) 6
Ship Inn, High Street East (No. 144) 13
Ship Isis, Silksworth Row 43
Ship Provident, Lombard Street 8
Ship Tavern, Lombard Street 8
Ship Tavern, Silksworth Row 43
Shipwrights Arms, Dame Dorothy Street 54
Shipwrights Arms, Rotherfield Road 66
Shoulder of Mutton, Ropery Lane 44
Sinatra's, Holmeside 36
Sir Colin Campbell, High Street East 10
Skiff Inn, Beach Street/Peacock Street 45, 48
Slipway, Blackwood Road 36, 65
Sloop, Lombard Street 8
Smiths Arms, Southwick Green 42, 62
Smugglers, Lower Promenade 60
Smyrna Hotel, South Durham Street 42
Sons of the Wear, Queen Street 34
Sportsman's Arms, Deptford Road 45
SR1, High Street West 37
St Peter's Wharf, Bonner's Field 55
Star Hotel, New Durham Road 42
Star Inn, High Street West 38
Station, Stoney Lane 63
Station Hotel, Moorgate Street 7
Station Hotel, Winchester Terrace 16
Stonebridge, Hylton Road 47
Stork, North Durham Street/Smryna Place 15
Strawberry Cottage, Tunstall Lane 19
Strokes, Hudson Road 20
Strutts, Low Row 33

Substance, Stockton Road 40
Sun Inn, Southwick Green 62
Sunderland Bridge, Lombard Street 8
Sunderland Flying Boat, Sea Road 61
Swallow Hotel, Queen's Parade 60
Swan Hotel, Henry Street 11

Tap and Barrel, Salem Street 20
Tap and Spile, Salem Street 20
Tatham Tavern, Tatham Street 20
Taylor's, Dovedale Road/Alston Crescent 61
Tea Shop, High Street West 38
Temple Bar, Coronation Street 8
Temple Bar, South Johnson Street 43
Terminus, Thomas Street 51
Theatre Tavern, Lambton Street 12, 21, 24
Thompson Arms, High Street East 3
Thorndale, Thorndale Road/Trent Road 48
Thorney Close, Thorndale Road 48
Three Crowns, High Street West 39
Three Tuns, Crowtree Road 28
Three Tuns, Moor Street 18
Times Inn, Wear Street 64
Toddy's, Ravenswood Road 66
Topsy's Happy Home, Lombard Street 8
Torrens, North Hylton Road 65
Traks, Holmeside 36
Tram Car, Southwick Green 62
Trimmers Arms, Pemberton Street 18
ttonic, Vine Place 37
Tunstall Lodge, Burdon Lane 19
Turf Hotel, West Wear Street 22, 25
Turk's Head, High Street East 10
Tyneside Castle, Moorgate Street 9-10

Underground, High Street West 41
Union Flag, Wear Street 55
Upper Deck, Walworth Way 26

Varsity, Green Terrace 33
Vestry, Fawcett Street 27
Victor Hotel, Victor Street 56
Victoria Gardens Hotel, China Street 20
Victoria Hotel, Fore Street 17
Victoria's, Low Row 33
Villiers Hotel, Villiers Street 21
Vine Cottage, Vine Place 30
Vision, Green Terrace 33
Vulcan Hotel, Millum Terrrace 57

Waggon Tavern, Brooke Street 52
Walton Hotel, Fawcett Street 27
Walworth Castle, Walworth Street 26
Waterman's Tavern, Fitters Row 10
Wavendon, Wavendon Crescent 38, 49
Waverley Hotel, Norman Street 23
Wear Inn, Wear Street 55
Wear Tavern, Long Bank 4, 10
Wearmouth Bridge, Thomas Street 51
Wearsider, Emsworth Road 65
Websters, Deptford Riverside 44
Welcome Tavern, Prospect Row 7, 9
Wellington Inn, Wellington Street 61, 63
Wessington, Wessington Way 65
West Country Arms, Ogle Street 64
Westbury Arms, Westbury Street 45
Wheat Sheaf, Moor Street 8
Wheat Sheaf, Johnson Street 43
Wheat Sheaf Hotel, Roker Avenue 58
White Hart, Queen Street 34
White House, Hendon Road 15
White Lion, High Street East 5
White Room, Holmeside 36
White Swan, High Street East 4
White Swan, Low Row 32
Whitwell Inn, Low Street 4
William IV, Lombard Street 8
William Jameson, Fawcett Street 36
William Pile, Dame Dorothy Street 57
Williamson Arms, Church Street 55
Willow Pond, Hylton Road 47
Windmills, Station Road 61
Windsor Castle, Nile Street 24
Winston, Hanover Place 44
Wolseley Hotel, Millum Terrace 59

Yates' Wine Lodge, Burdon House 36
Ye Olde Friendly Tavern, Southwick Road 62
Ye Olde Transporter, Low Row 32